AN AMBITION FOR EQUALITY

JUSTICE IN CONTROVERSY SERIES

Editors: Mike Milotte and Donncha O'Connell

This series of monographs will address a range of controversial legal topics in a format that will appeal to audiences beyond the purely professional and academic legal worlds. It will be written by a combination of established and emerging authors with legal, academic, journalistic and other backgrounds. By virtue of their subject-matter on the interaction between law and society, the books will inform academic debate; but, given the profound and enduring effect of the law on the lives of all citizens, it is also envisaged that the books will have a much wider appeal and impact. The series aims to provide a distinctive contribution to public discourse by providing a publishing platform for authors that wish to transcend the rather exclusive borders that separate public and academic discourse.

Forthcoming in the Justice in Controversy series:

The Blame Game: Rethinking Ireland's Sustainable Development and Environmental Performance, by Brendan Flynn

Whittling the 'Golden Thread': the Presumption of Innocence and Irish Criminal Law, by Claire Hamilton

Tough Lives, Rough Justice: A Critical Analysis of Juvenile Justice In Ireland, by Ursula Kilkelly

Roadmaps to Reunification, by Richard Humphreys

Exploitation or Employment? Prostitution and the Law, by Ivana Bacik

The Future of Irish Nationality and Immigration Law, by Bernard Ryan

AN AMBITION
FOR
EQUALITY

Niall Crowley

IRISH ACADEMIC PRESS
DUBLIN • PORTLAND, OR

First published in 2006 by
IRISH ACADEMIC PRESS
44, Northumberland Road, Dublin 4, Ireland

and in the United States of America by
IRISH ACADEMIC PRESS
c/o ISBS, Suite 300, 920 NE 58th Avenue
Portland, Oregon 97213-3644

© 2006 Niall Crowley

WEBSITE:iap.ie

British Library Cataloguing in Publication Data
An entry can be found on request

ISBN 0-7165-3381-2 (cloth)
ISBN 0-7165-3382-0 (paper)

Library of Congress Cataloging-in-Publication Data
An entry can be found on request

Typeset in 11/13pt Sabon by FiSH Books, Enfield, Middx.

Printed by MPG Books Ltd, Bodmin, Cornwall

An Ambition for Equality is dedicated to
Melanie Reidy, who gave me my first lessons on
gender equality, and to Liam Reidy and
Lorcan Reidy who so generously and supportively
shared the kitchen table with the book for so long.

Contents

Acknowledgements

An Ambition for Equality draws heavily on my learning since becoming Chief Executive Officer of the Equality Authority. I am grateful to all my colleagues in the Equality Authority. Their commitment and expertise have contributed so much to this learning.

I am also grateful to the chairperson, Karen Erwin, and the Board of the Equality Authority, for their positive response to my taking on of the writing of this book.

I am particularly grateful to Eilis Barry, who read both drafts of the book and provided insightful and valuable commentary each time.

Thanks are due to Pat Hogan and Ann Ross for her patient work in putting in the final edits.

Finally, I am grateful to Mike Milotte and Donncha O'Connell, series editors, for their invitation to write and for their support in finalising the text.

Foreword

The name of Niall Crowley has become synonymous with the search for equality in Ireland. In that work he has perhaps attracted as many brickbats as bouquets, not an uncommon experience for those who cause discomfort to vested interests, whether these are material, political or social.

In this book, which is to be the first of a new monograph series entitled 'Justice in Controversy', Niall Crowley analyses the concept of equality, its core dimensions and the role played by non-governmental organisations, the political parties and the social partners in the promotion of equality in society. In his Introduction he provides a clear and concise history of the growth of equality legislation and the institutions promoting equality from the enactment of the Anti-Discrimination (Pay) Act 1974 to the present. In later chapters he explores his vision for a more equal society, the role of the Equality Authority as an institution, the developments of equality legislation and of practices designed to promote equality, including targeting and mainstreaming.

The author rightly describes equality as *'a contested concept'*. While there may be a shared concern at the persistence of inequalities and agreement on the need for a change in the economic, political, cultural and caring domains, there still remains a contest of ideas about how far society needs to go or should go in terms of the level of equality sought and in terms of the mechanisms that can be deployed to achieve this level of equality. Liberal egalitarianism which emphasises non-discrimination and equality of opportunity is, he believes, not enough because it can accept and co-exist with significant levels of inequality. Tolerance of difference has its virtues but it can too readily co-exist with ignorance and even contempt. A more positive approach is needed, aimed at what Mr Crowley describes as '*equality of condition*'.

The final chapter of his book is entitled *Backlash – A Faltering Ambition*. By way of illustration quotations are given from some of the more abusive media attacks on both the Equality Authority and on the whole concept of equality, written by opinion columnists who are unlikely to have experience of the sharp end of discrimination. These writers illustrate the more extreme end of opposition to an equality agenda. Nevertheless, Mr Crowley is right in believing that, while there is not widespread actual opposition, there is what might be described as a fading of enthusiasm for the active promotion of equality across all the sectors included in the more recent equality legislation. This is a common experience in movements for change and reform where it has become a widely held, if erroneous, belief that the main objects of the movement have already been achieved. It is all too easy for this to give rise to an accusation that 'the pendulum has swung too far'. Those who have experienced over the years the movement for gender equality must have some sympathy for Mr Crowley here.

The author concludes that while important progress has been made in constructing and applying a strategic framework for action on equality, inequality continues to be the experience in reality for a broad range of groups. However there has been no faltering of ambition for equality among those who experience inequality and this ambition is fuelled by anger and frustration. He seeks the creation of a culture where it is deemed normal to seek to demand and exercise one's rights and the creation of new strategies for action on the promotion of equality.

This is a valuable and comprehensive work which provides analysis and insight across the equality agenda. It is an encouraging start for the new series to be published by the Irish Academic Press.

CATHERINE McGUINNESS
September 2005

Introduction

New Legislation and New Institutions

'Discrimination in whatever form demands, I repeat demands, a proactive approach by the State', stated Taoiseach, Bertie Ahern TD in October 1999. He was speaking at an event to mark the enactment of the Employment Equality Act 1998 and the establishment of the Equality Authority and of the Office of the Director of Equality Investigations (ODEI) (later to be known as the Equality Tribunal). He stated: 'This legislation will work if Irish people want it to work and those of us in leadership, in the media, in public life – in all of society – need to understand that. We all need to accept our responsibility to make sure that it does work and brings about change and an end to discrimination.'

In October 2000, the Minister for Justice Equality and Law Reform John O'Donoghue TD, expressed his ambition for equality in these terms: 'Equality for people is about having the same rights and the same chances and everyone has an equal right to participate in our community.' He also stated that Ireland now had 'what many commentators regard as the most comprehensive and progressive anti-discrimination legislation in the EU'. He was speaking at an event to mark the enactment of the Equal Status Act 2000.

The new legislation and the new institutions marked a new ambition for equality. Prior to this, equality legislation was confined to workplace issues and was limited to the grounds of gender and marital status. The relevant legislation was the Anti-Discrimination (Pay) Act 1974, which established an entitlement to equal pay between men and women, and the Employment

Equality Act 1977, which prohibited discrimination by employers on grounds of sex and marital status in relation to access to employment, training or experience, promotion or re-grading. These Acts had their origins in requirements accompanying Ireland's membership of the European Union. Ireland was going beyond any European Union requirements with this new equality legislation to assume a leadership role on equality legislation within the European Union.

This leadership is based on legislation and institutions that sought to be comprehensive and holistic in combating discrimination and promoting equality. The legislation sought to be comprehensive in prohibiting discrimination across nine grounds. Both the Employment Equality Act 1998 and the Equal Status Act 2000 prohibit discrimination on the grounds of gender, marital status, family status, age, disability, sexual orientation, race, religion and membership of the Traveller community.

The Acts sought to be holistic in relation to organisations by addressing both the human resource and customer service functions of organisations. The Employment Equality Act 1998 prohibits discrimination in access to employment, terms and conditions of employment, vocational training and work experience, promotion, collective agreements and advertising. The Equal Status Act 2000 prohibits discrimination in the provision of goods and services, accommodation and educational establishments. It contains separate provisions in relation to registered clubs.

The Acts established the Equality Authority and the Office of the Director of Equality Investigations (Equality Tribunal), each with a mandate that covers all nine grounds and both of the Acts. The Equality Authority is accorded an ambitious mandate under the legislation to work towards the elimination of discrimination and the promotion of equality of opportunity in the areas that are the subject of the two Acts. The Office of the Director of Equality Investigations (Equality Tribunal) is a separate and distinct organisation. There has been some confusion in this regard. It is a quasi-judicial body established to mediate or investigate, hear and decide claims made under the Acts. The District Court, the Labour Court and the Circuit Court are also accorded roles under the Acts.

WHERE DID THE NEW EQUALITY LEGISLATION COME FROM?

The significance of this new legislation and the scale of the change it reflected can be gauged from a brief consideration of its historical context. The 'marriage bar' was still in effect in the early 1970s. This required women working in the civil service, including state and semi state bodies, to leave their jobs once they got married. It was not until 1989 that it was made legal for unmarried people to buy condoms. It was only after a significant public campaign and lobby work that Travellers were included in the Prohibition of Incitement to Hatred Act 1989. Homosexuality was decriminalized in 1993 in response to a case taken by David Norris to the European Court of Human Rights. As late as 1995 the Commission on the Status of People with Disabilities reported that 'people with disabilities are the neglected citizens of Ireland' and that 'public attitudes towards disability are still based on charity rather than on rights'.[1] It was only in the late 1990s that the demands of the economy required the presence of significant numbers of migrant workers which further broadened the cultural diversity in society. This was also a period which witnessed a decline in the authority of the Catholic Church and a growth in the diversity of Churches present and religious faiths being practised in Ireland. The stimulus for the significant development reflected in the new equality legislation involved all of the key actors in the search for a more equal society – non-governmental organisations, political parties and the social partners.

Non-governmental organisations

In 1990 the Irish Council for Civil Liberties published *Equality Now for Lesbians and Gay Men*. This made the case for anti-discrimination legislation 'to encode an open-ended prohibition against discrimination on the basis of sexual orientation combined with a list of specific forms of prohibited discrimination'. It provided a draft for 'elements of a model equality (anti-discrimination) Bill'. It is of interest that this was posed in an integrated context that included the grounds of 'race, religion, colour, ethnic origin (including membership of the Travelling community), gender, family status, health disability'.[2]

In 1990 Nelson Mandela came to Dublin. Traveller groups sought to 'highlight some of the parallels between the treatment of Black people in South Africa and of the Travellers in Ireland'.[3] The occasion provided an opportunity to highlight discrimination experienced by Travellers as well as to express solidarity with South Africa. Later in the year controversy arose in 'Glenroe'. This happened after the shooting of a wedding scene for the popular television soap. In the episode Travellers were refused service of drink. After filming had finished the management of a Co. Wicklow pub refused to serve the Travellers who had acted as extras in the scene. Traveller groups used the incident to highlight their demand for anti-discrimination legislation.

Over the early 1990s Traveller groups highlighted incidents of discrimination by public houses, local authorities, schools and insurance companies to establish the need for such legislation. In 1993 the Dublin Traveller Education and Development Group, the Irish Council for Civil Liberties and the Irish Traveller Movement published *Anti-Racist Law and the Travellers*. This made the case for legislation to address discrimination in a manner that would 'go beyond punishment of individual acts of discrimination. It must also deal with the structural nature of discrimination through a focus on institutional policy and practice and a commitment to affirmative action to redress past discrimination'.[4] The publication stressed that 'Effective legislation requires independent infrastructure to ensure its implementation' and again made the case for a broad approach 'prohibiting discrimination against all groups who have traditionally been subject to oppressive power and social prejudice'. A draft Equality Bill was presented to 'protect minority ethnic groups and groups suffering discrimination on the basis of skin colour'.

Women's organisations and disability organisations were also highlighting the need for such legislation. These groups came together with gay and lesbian organisations and Traveller groups to form an equality coalition to campaign for effective anti-discrimination legislation. This was an important development in establishing shared concerns across the different grounds and in building a consensus across the grounds as to how these concerns might best be resolved. This cooperation raised the issue of the intersections between the grounds. Each ground is made up of a diversity that includes all the other grounds. The National Women's Council of Ireland in particular had a focus in their work on the diversity of women as, for example, women with disabilities, lesbian women and Traveller women.

The non-governmental organisations publicly articulated the different experiences of discrimination. They made the demand for change in this experience and set out a range of approaches through which such change could be achieved. They built a broad constituency to give voice to this demand for change.

Political Parties

The political parties were central in responding to this demand for change. The political will for greater equality that emerged over the 1990s was key in the development of the equality legislation that took place. This was given specific expression by what was a unique coalition in Irish political terms in 1993. The Fianna Fáil and Labour political parties produced a Programme for Government that included a commitment to 'eliminating inequality for all groups in society that have suffered from disability, disadvantage or discrimination'.[5] This committed both parties to pursuing equality legislation making discrimination unlawful in the workplace and in the provision of goods and services across a broad range of grounds. This led to the publication of the Employment Equality Bill 1996 and the Equal Status Bill 1997. Both Bills were passed by the Dáil and Seanad. However, they were subsequently referred to the Supreme Court by the then President Mary Robinson where elements of the legislation were found to run counter to the Constitution.

The judgment of the Supreme Court diminished the level of ambition in this equality legislation. This diminution related in particular to provisions on the disability ground. The requirements established by the legislation in relation to employers and service providers making adjustments to reasonably accommodate people with disabilities were found to be unconstitutional. Primacy was accorded by the Supreme Court to private property guarantees in the Constitution. The subsequent revision of the legislation included a significantly reduced requirement in relation to reasonable accommodation of people with disabilities on employers and service providers.

The need to revise the equality legislation on foot of this judgment resulted in a situation that ultimately reflected a broad political consensus behind the new equality legislation. It fell to a new coalition to start work on revising the legislation on foot of the Supreme Court decision. This involved the Fine Gael, Labour and Democratic Left political parties. The final enactment of the new legislation was the work of yet another coalition involving the Fianna Fáil and Progressive Democrat political parties. All political parties represented in the Dáil, with the exception of the Green Party and Sinn Féin who were not in Government over this period, played an active part in bringing forward the new equality legislation.

Social Partners

The final set of organisations that can be identified as part of the stimulus for change are the social partners. This involves not only the traditional social partners, the Irish Congress of Trade Unions (Congress) and the Irish Business and Employers Confederation (IBEC), but the wider configuration of organisations involved in the four pillars within social partnership that were put in place during the 1990s – business, trade union, farming and community and voluntary pillars. The community and voluntary pillar was the most recent to be established. It included organisations articulating the interests of women, older people, people with disabilities, Travellers, lone parents, gay and lesbian people and young people.

The social partners contribute, through the various arenas of social partnership, to all stages of the policy cycle – policy thinking, policy making and policy implementation. Policy thinking emphasises the ideas, concepts, values and strategies that underpin policy making. The National Economic and Social Council (NESC) involves the social partners along with civil servants in policy thinking with its mandate to 'provide a forum for discussion of the principles relating to the efficient development of the national economy and the achievement of social justice and to advise the government through the Taoiseach on their application'.[6]

The social partners have engaged with government in the negotiation of national agreements since 1987. These have always been more than agreements on pay and conditions of employment. They also include a wide range of commitments to social policy issues – including equality issues. The national agreements involve the social parties in policy making.

The National Economic and Social Forum (NESF) involves the social partners alongside politicians and civil servants in a focus on policy implementation issues. Its mandate includes 'to monitor and analyse the implementation of specific measures and programmes identified, especially those concerned with the achievement of equality and social inclusion'.[7]

In February 1996 the National Economic and Social Forum produced a groundbreaking report entitled 'Equality Proofing Issues'. This report made specific recommendations on the content of employment equality and equal status legislation. It highlighted the need to establish equality objectives that focus on 'seeking to achieve equality of access, participation and outcome'.[8] This reflected a new level of shared and agreed ambition for equality with its focus on outcomes achieved for groups experiencing inequality. This goes beyond the previous emphasis on equality of opportunity. The report recommended the adoption of equality proofing arrangements and procedures in assessing the impact of government policies and programmes and the encouragement of equality proofing administrative procedures in the private and voluntary and community sectors.

This report has underpinned a significant ambition for equality among the social partners that has continued to find expression in national agreements. It is reflected in the contribution made by the social partners across the different arenas of social partnership to negotiating new thinking, new policy and new practice to shape a more equal society. It is evident in the developing understanding of the strategic framework for equality articulated in NESC reports, national agreements and NESF reports.

An Ambition for Equality

A STRATEGIC FRAMEWORK FOR ACTION ON EQUALITY

The Partnership 2000 for Inclusion Employment and Competitiveness national agreement was agreed later in 1996. For the first time the negotiation included a community and voluntary pillar. This agreement committed the government to employment equality and equal status legislation alongside 'the strengthening of administrative procedures for equality proofing' in the context of the National Anti Poverty Strategy. It established that 'it is an objective of this partnership to develop a strategy which enhances equality and counters discrimination in both employment and non employment areas'.[9]

The agreement opened up the concept of a strategic approach to equality that would include but go beyond provisions made in equality legislation. This concept was further developed by the National Economic and Social Council in its report *Opportunities, Challenges and Capacities for Choice*. In this report 'the council reiterates and reinforces its support for the enhancement of equality through the promotion of equality of opportunity, participation and outcome as a positive good'. It argues that 'public policy is an essential mechanism for combating discrimination and enhancing equality' and 'the council supports the creation of a strategic framework for action on equality which would include the comprehensive strategic implementation of the recommendations of past/current equality agendas and the development of equality agendas for the legislatively new groups experiencing discrimination'.[10]

The Programme for Prosperity and Fairness was negotiated on foot of this strategy report. This agreed five equality related objectives. These included 'to create a fair and inclusive society by putting in place a strategic framework for action on equality in accordance with the NESC Strategy Document'.[11] It was not until March 2002 that the social partners set out a comprehensive and agreed position on what should be involved in a strategic framework for action on equality. This was done in a report of the National Economic and Social Forum, *A Strategic Policy Framework for Equality Issues*.

This report set out that the strategic framework should involve:

- a vision for a more equal society that incorporates all nine grounds of the new equality agenda;
- equality objectives derived from a current analysis of equality issues; and
- seven core dimensions through which activity can be delivered to achieve these equality objectives.[12]

The report went on to identify these core dimensions and make recommendations in relation to each. The seven core dimensions are identified as:

- legislation – this referred in particular to equality legislation to combat discrimination and promote equality.
- institutions – this referred to the organisations established to implement the equality legislation. It also referred to the contribution to be made to promoting equality by all organisations with responsibilities for implementing public policy.
- mainstreaming – this referred to the processes necessary to ensure that policies, programmes and practices of all public bodies contributed to the goal of equality.
- targeting – this referred to investment of resources to address the impact of discrimination on particular groups, to provide for needs that might be specific to particular groups and to support outcomes from mainstream provision for groups experiencing inequality.
- participation – this referred in particular to the inclusion of organisations articulating the interests of those experiencing inequality in decision making.
- agenda setting – this referred to the need to develop agendas for changing the experience and situation of those groups which experience inequality.
- monitoring – this referred in particular to gathering and analysing data in relation to those groups experiencing inequality.

AN AMBITION FOR EQUALITY

An Ambition for Equality is the title of this publication. The enactment of the equality legislation described earlier in this chapter identifies a moment of significant ambition for equality. However an analysis of equality issues put forward in subsequent chapters suggests that this ambition for equality has not been as evident in the development and implementation of a wider response to current inequalities. The concluding chapter will identify a significant faltering in this ambition for equality since the enactment of the equality legislation.

A focus throughout the publication on the strategic framework for action on equality provides an opportunity to raise and explore a broad range of equality issues. It allows an examination of the current ambition for equality in Irish society to the extent that this is reflected in mechanisms and initiatives put in place to bring forward and address issues of inequality and discrimination. It provides a means to identify further developments required to create a more equal society.

Chapter One explores a vision for a more equal society. It examines different understandings of equality, the rationale for action on equality, current experiences of inequality, and the objectives for a strategic framework for action on equality. Subsequent chapters explore some of the core dimensions to this strategic framework through which activity can be pursued to achieve these equality objectives. Chapter Two explores the role of the Equality Authority as an institution within the strategic framework in seeking change through enforcement of the legislation, through negotiation and joint action with other institutions, through cultural action and communication initiatives and through knowledge development and research. Chapter Three explores the provisions of the equality legislation, the patterns of discrimination that are evident from casework under the legislation, the developments in the legislation since its enactment and perspectives on the further development of the legislation. Chapter Four explores the importance of targeting resources on groups experiencing inequality and the pitfalls that can be associated with targeting. It explores the need for a dual strategy of targeting and mainstreaming and the approaches to mainstreaming that are emerging. Chapter Five explores the concept of equality competence and the practices developed by institutions that seek to be equality competent. A final chapter seeks to summarise progress in developing this strategic framework for action on equality.

An Ambition for Equality is written in a personal capacity. The views expressed are those of the author alone. However it is based on the author's ongoing experience and position as chief executive officer of the Equality Authority. This informs and shapes the personal perspectives put forward in this publication just as it sets boundaries to these. The work of the Equality Authority, due to its broad mandate, provides a valuable lens through which to view and explore the strategic framework for action on equality and this is the approach taken in this publication.

This personal perspective is informed by a commitment to contributing to developing a society and institutions within society where:

- discrimination is eliminated and where steps are taken to ensure experiences of discrimination cannot arise;
- diversity in identities, experiences and situation of groups is acknowledged and valued as a source of creativity and development, and the practical implications of such diversity are taken into account;
- full equality in practice is pursued as an objective for all groups experiencing inequality with positive action deployed as appropriate and necessary.

NOTES

1. *A Strategy for Equality*, Report of the Commission on the Status of People with Disabilities, Stationery Office (Dublin) 1995
2. *Equality Now for Lesbians and Gay Men*, Irish Council for Civil Liberties (Dublin) 1990
3. *Worlds Apart?*, Dublin Travellers Education and Development Group (Dublin) 1990
4. *Anti-Racist Law and Travellers*, Dublin Travellers Education and Development Group, Irish Council for Civil Liberties, Irish Traveller Movement (Dublin) 1993
5. *Fianna Fáil and Labour Programme for a Partnership Government 1993-97*
6. *Opportunities, Challenges and Capacities for Choice*, National Economic and Social Council (Dublin) 1999
7. *A Strategic Policy Framework for Equality Issues*, National Economic and Social Forum (Dublin) 2002
8. *Equality Proofing Issues*, Forum Report No. 10 National Economic and Social Forum (Dublin) 1996
9. *Partnership 2000 for Inclusion Employment and Competitiveness*, The Stationery Office (Dublin) 1996
10. *Opportunities, Challenges and Capacities for Choice*, National Economic and Social Council (Dublin) 1999
11. *Programme for Prosperity and Fairness*, The Stationery Office (Dublin) 1999.
12. *A Strategic Policy Framework for Equality Issues*, National Economic and Social Forum (Dublin) 2002

Chapter One

Equality

A vision for a more equal society is the starting point for a strategic framework for action on equality.[1] The ambition within this vision and the quality of analysis that informs it will significantly affect the potential impact of the various dimensions to the strategic framework such as institutions, legislation, mainstreaming and targeting. This chapter seeks to explore this concept of a vision for a more equal society and in doing so establishes an understanding of equality that is used throughout this publication. It starts with an examination of the rationale for a commitment to equality.

This rationale can be found in the culture or value base of society. It can be seen in the economic and political imperatives of a society. Thus there is a diversity of reasons – cultural, economic and political – to be concerned about equality. This diversity is valuable where different groups and interests in society can be inspired and mobilised by a concern for equality for different reasons. It is a diversity that holds the potential for building a wide consensus for a more equal society.

Equality has a cultural rationale. It can be identified as part of the value base of a society. Equality involves placing a value on people as human beings. At its core, equality is about equal human worth.

Many academic commentators have highlighted this emphasis on human worth as a key starting point for a concern for equality. In *Equality – From Theory to Action* Baker, Lynch,

Cantillon and Walsh, from the inter-disciplinary Equality Studies Centre in University College Dublin, suggest that 'basic equality is the cornerstone of all egalitarian thinking: the idea that at some very basic level all human beings have equal worth and importance, and are therefore equally worthy of concern and respect'.[2] In her publication, *Which Equalities Matter*, Anne Phillips, a professor of Gender Theory, writes of 'political equality understood not only as the equal right to participate in politics but as that deeper notion of equal intrinsic worth'.[3] In *Charting the Equality Agenda* Katherine Zappone, a social policy research consultant, highlights that 'cultural equality requires, at the outset, a fundamental acknowledgement of the diverse ways of being human'.[4]

The broad subscription to this cultural rationale for equality is evidenced in the Irish Constitution. Article 40.1 states that 'All citizens shall, as human persons, be held equal before the law.' This equality guarantee is linked to the value placed on human worth by the reference to 'as human persons'. The shared nature of this value base was further emphasised in the recent negotiations for a new constitution for the European Union. The proposed constitution identifies equality as a value of the European Union. Article 1.2 states that the European Union is 'founded on values of respect for human dignity, liberty, democracy, equality, the rule of law and respect for human rights'. The broad range of United Nations conventions – on civil and political rights, on social and economic rights, on the elimination of discrimination against women, and on the elimination of all forms of racial discrimination – identify that this value base for equality is a global phenomenon rather than anything unique to Ireland or the European Union.

An economic rationale for equality can be identified. Equality involves removing the barriers faced by particular groups in seeking access to work, to an income and to a wider set of resources. In this way equality enables everyone to make their contribution as employees, entrepreneurs and paying consumers to economic development. Equality involves the elimination of poverty. In this way equality contributes to significant savings in the human and financial costs associated with the experience and impact of poverty.

This economic rationale for equality is increasingly evident in mainstream economic strategies. In September 2003 a meeting of the OECD Employment and Labour Ministers concluded that 'more policy attention should also be devoted to mobilising under-represented groups into jobs and helping them realise their career potential. Success on these fronts would improve employment performance and social cohesion and help safeguard future living standards and the sustainability of our welfare systems.'[5] Equality within the labour market has emerged as a significant focus as economic growth is threatened by labour shortages. Those groups which have previously experienced significant distance from and inequality within the labour market find a more positive response to their search for inclusion and equality through paid employment.

This economic rationale for equality is evident in the European Employment Strategy. This strategy was launched at the Luxembourg Council in 1997. Member States are required to prepare and implement annual national employment action plans. These are based on common guidelines agreed at European Union level by the Member States. Up until 2005 the employment strategy guidelines required the employment policies of the Member States to work towards the objectives of full employment, quality and productivity at work, and social cohesion and inclusion. The guidelines emphasised that equality is a central component of all three objectives: 'equal opportunities and gender equality are vital for making progress towards the three objectives.'[6]

Equality is underpinned by a political rationale. Equality involves an inclusion for all groups in decision making. This broad inclusion underpins a democratic legitimacy as all groups are enabled to have a sense of ownership of societal institutions. It supports a quality in decision making that is based on access to the information and knowledge made available by this diversity of groups.

It is not surprising to find equality highlighted as a value in the proposed European Union Constitution. Democratic legitimacy is a challenge for the European institutions given their distance from the individual citizens. A commitment to equality is an important element of a wider commitment by the European institutions to be relevant to the experience and situation of the individual citizen. The incorporation of this commitment to equality into the Constitution provides a legal basis for the EU to take action on equality issues and to enhance the situation and experience of its citizens in this regard.

Equality therefore is an expression of the value placed on human worth by society. It is identified as an important factor in the success of strategies for economic development. It is seen to contribute to the legitimacy of democratic institutions. This represents a powerful and diverse rationale for equality with a capacity to inspire and mobilise a broad range of interests in society. With such a rationale established the next issue that needs exploration is who is identified as a focus for this broad concern for equality.

EQUALITY FOR WHOM?

Current equality debates emphasise the context of difference and diversity in the make-up of society. Phillips refers to the 'new preoccupation with equality under conditions of difference' and 'the shift in attention from class inequalities that undermine democracy to the gender, racial or cultural hierarchies that subvert equal citizenship'.[7] This shift has been important in focusing attention on the wider range of inequalities experienced by a broad diversity of groups. It has been limiting in that it has not included a focus on inequalities experienced on the basis of socio-economic status.

Irish equality legislation reflects this emphasis on difference and diversity. The grounds covered by the legislation are gender, marital status, family status, age, disability, sexual orientation, race, religion and membership of the Traveller community. The legislation, with its coverage of nine grounds stimulates and underpins a welcome and important breadth to equality strategies. The nine grounds emphasise difference and diversity in terms of identity. Membership of groups within most of the grounds is innate rather than by choice or circumstance. Identity flows from a range of sources. These sources include one's gender, age, disability, ethnicity, skin colour, nationality, sexual identity and religion. Identity also flows from and can be partly shaped by experiences shared by the group of discrimination and exclusion – experiences of sexism, ageism, disabilism, racism, homophobia or sectarianism. Groups characterised by a shared identity which is in part shaped by experiences of discrimination and exclusion are an important focus for equality strategies.

Groups characterised by status, which is not innate but flows from circumstances or choice, can also be an important focus for equality strategies. The nine grounds cover marital status and family status which includes some of these groups. Socio-economic status is one significant absence from this broad breadth of approach to equality. The equality legislation affords no protection for discrimination on the basis of socio-economic status. This perhaps reflects a reluctance to address a wider economic dimension to current inequalities. It leaves a significant and large group of people without access to legal redress for the discrimination they can experience. It contributes to a fragmentation between anti-poverty and equality strategies.

Equality is promoted through equality legislation. Poverty is combated through a National Anti-Poverty Strategy. The Equality Authority is established to promote equality and combat discrimination. The Combat Poverty Agency is established to contribute to eliminating poverty. This fragmentation can limit a response to the significant interface between poverty and inequality. Many of the groups covered by the equality legislation also experience poverty. Lone parents, Travellers, people with disabilities and older people are all target groups for anti-poverty measures. Many of the other target groups for anti-poverty measures include a diversity of people from across the grounds covered by equality legislation. Homeless people for example include men and women, gay and lesbian people, people with disabilities and people from minority ethnic groups. This diversity has practical implications for anti-poverty measures targeting homelessness. This fragmentation of anti-poverty and equality strategies can limit the impact of measures taken to address poverty or measures taken to promote equality.

Equality therefore, in the current strategic framework for action on equality, has a particular focus on grounds characterised by a diversity of identities. There is a need to further develop this focus to include all groups that experience inequality. It is useful now to identify the situations of inequality within these nine grounds. Exploring these inequalities will assist in defining objectives for equality strategies.

INEQUALITY

The situation of groups within the nine grounds covered by the equality legislation demonstrates significant inequalities. A brief sketch serves to illustrate this situation. A number of the issues are further developed in subsequent chapters.

Women's hourly earnings are 82.5% of men's.[8] Only 40% or so of those reporting a long-standing/chronic illness or disability were in employment compared to 70% for other adults of working age.[9] Migrant workers report experiences of low pay and poor working conditions.[10] In the 1996 census only 9% of Travellers are identified as being in mainstream employment.[11] In terms of employment, older people are over represented in declining sectors such as agriculture.[12] Carers experience significant difficulties in reconciling paid employment and caring responsibilities.[13]

Travellers report low attendance, early dropout and low educational attainment in education.[14] Sixty-three per cent of older people (55 to 64 years old) hold less than upper second level qualifications compared to 45% among 15 to 64 year olds.[15] Early school leaving rates are higher among boys than among girls.[16] Segregated education provision continues for children with disabilities and students with disabilities are underrepresented at third level.[17]

Women have a greater life expectancy than men.[18] Older people have uneven access to health services in Ireland.[19] The life expectancy of Travellers is considerably below the national average and infant mortality rates among the Traveller community are over twice those of the settled community.[20] Health services to provide a treatment path for transsexual people are underdeveloped.[21]

In 2003 there was a total of 1,738 Traveller families with no permanent accommodation which accounted for 30% of all Traveller families.[22] Some Black and minority ethnic people find it difficult to secure private rented accommodation due to high costs, reluctance by some landlords to accept rent allowance, language barriers and/or discrimination.[23] Housing disadvantage or deprivation is more common among older people.[24]

Ireland has the eighth lowest proportion of women in parliament of the twenty-five EU Members States at 13.3%.[25] People with disabilities, Travellers and other minority ethnic people are largely absent from most arenas of representative democracy. This pattern is repeated across private and public sector organisations at Board level and in senior management positions.[26]

The built environment and many manufactured products have not been designed to take account of the needs of people with disabilities. Partnership rights are not available to gay and lesbian people leaving them with no legal recognition for their relationships.[27] A culture of disrespect for difference is evident in educational establishments.[28] Under the current law in Ireland there is no provision allowing transsexual people to be officially recognised in the gender with which they identify.[29] Traveller nomadism has not been facilitated by a network of transient sites as recommended by the Task Force on the Travelling Community.[30]

Personal safety in a context of physical and verbal abuse is an issue for women, Black and minority ethnic people including Travellers, gay and lesbian people, older people and people with disability.[31] The Dochas Dingle Men's Action Group identifies the experience of men living alone on the Dingle peninsula in terms of isolation and of the absence of social contact on any regular basis.[32] Carers identify experiences of isolation and lack of social contact in a context of underdeveloped support services.[33] Less than 1% of those declaring their primary role as looking after home/family in 2001 were men.[34] In 2002 it was reported that 84% of parental leave taken was taken by women.[35]

Common threads can be identified in these situations of the different groups. It is useful to identify these common threads to assist in defining equality objectives. Inequalities are evident in the economic, political, cultural and caring domains. Economic equalities are identified in employment and income. They are also evident in access to a wider range of resources such as education, health and accommodation. Political inequalities are identified in relation to access to the institutions of representative democracy. They are also evident in relation to access to decision-making positions across a broad range of societal institutions. Cultural inequalities are identified in the failure to accommodate or make provision for diversity and the practical implications of different identities. Caring inequalities are identified in experiences of hostility and abuse and of isolation and limited social contact. They are also evident in terms of which groups predominantly play caring roles. These common threads provide the basis for an interlinked set of equality objectives that encompass the economic, political, cultural and caring domains.

EQUALITY OBJECTIVES

Equality objectives need to be established in a manner that responds to the breadth of situations of inequality identified in the previous section. These equality objectives will therefore be focused on economic equality, political equality, cultural equality and caring equality. These different equality objectives need to be inter-linked to achieve a holistic response to the situation of groups experiencing inequality.

Economic Equality

Economic equality involves an equality in access to and distribution of resources. Resources include income and wealth as well as employment and resources for economic development. They encompass key social goods such as health, education and accommodation. Economic equality has a broad remit and a central importance when seen in this way. Phillips highlights that 'most struggles for equality will depend on some modification of social conditions'.[36] Baker *et al.* establish the importance of moving the focus beyond income and wealth to include 'a number of other goods that people find useful in achieving their life's aims'.[37] Zappone suggests that one way 'in which economic equality matters has to do with establishing the conditions for people's freedom to develop their capacities'.[38]

The objective of economic equality will involve a significant redistribution of resources in society. It should not be defined however as some form of mathematical equality. It will rather be concerned with meaningful choices and the freedom and capacity to make such choices between real options. When people make such choices a diversity of outcomes emerge. As Phillips highlights: 'since individuals do have some choices about and responsibility for their economic actions, this means I do not defend strict equality of outcome.'[39]

The objective of economic equality will further be concerned with breaking current linkages between group membership and inequality and poverty. Economic equality will contribute to dismantling structures and systems that create these permanent hierarchies between groups. Again, however, this is not to be understood as everyone being the same. Baker et al highlight that such equality 'cannot be equated with the idea that everyone should have the same income and wealth, because people have different needs and because there are so many important resources to consider'. They pose the objective in terms of 'people's overall resources are much more equal than they are now'.[40]

Economic equality will influence the achievement of the wider set of objectives for equality. Access to resources can be linked to access to participation in decision making. How one is valued is at times linked to resources. Social contact may depend on access to resources. Conversely, while economic equality is important in and of itself, it can be supported, shaped and enhanced by equality in the political, cultural and caring spheres.

Political Equality

Political equality involves access to decision making. It involves access to and participation in, the democratic institutions of society, alongside a wider participation for groups experiencing inequality in decision making in the workplace and in the provision of public sector goods and services. It involves participation in decision making in the full range of institutions in any society whether they are deemed to be in a private or a public realm. Phillips poses this in terms of 'approaching an equality of influence'.[41]

Political equality is enhanced where a participatory model of democracy operates alongside the current model of representative democracy. A participatory model of democracy is where people are directly engaged in decision making that impacts on them. This is particularly important in a context where minority groups do not have the numbers sufficient to secure a representation of their specific interests in arenas of representative democracy. Participatory models of democracy can include institutions specifically to hear and engage with the voice of those who experience inequality. In an Irish context the development of social partnership institutions and processes at national, local and enterprise levels provides a basis for participatory democracy. Community organisations that identify, articulate and negotiate the interests of different groups experiencing inequality are an important participant in social partnership institutions and processes. This model of social partnership reflects one initial response to the challenge posed by Baker *et al.* for 'a more participatory form of politics in which ordinary citizens, and particularly groups who have been excluded from power altogether, can have more control over decision making'.[42]

Equality in access to decision making also involves a broader participation in the arenas of representative democracy. The diversity of society needs to be better reflected in the composition of these key decision making arenas. A diversity of voices will ensure a visibility for the needs of different groups in society within these arenas. Diversity in the make-up of these arenas will bring a wider range of experiences, information and knowledge to their deliberations. This will enhance the quality of decision making. This objective of political equality has not proven a simple challenge in relation to achieving equality in the participation of women in these arenas of representative democracy. It becomes even more challenging in terms of achieving equal access for minority groups in these arenas.

The participation by members of a diversity of groups in decision making needs to extend beyond the institutions of representative or participatory democracy. The same diversity needs to be present across senior management in the public and private sectors. It is needed in the judiciary, and within the legal and other professions. It is needed within cultural and media institutions. This participation is needed because it will provide role models for groups experiencing inequality. It will challenge stereotyping of and false assumptions about these groups. It will secure a societal leadership that reflects the perspectives and interests of all groups in society.

Schools could be one important training ground for new models of decision making that are more inclusive. The reliance in schools on traditional models of authoritarian and exclusive leadership must therefore be a source of concern. Lynch, a professor of Equality Studies, and Lodge, a lecturer in the sociology of education, explored this issue.[43] They found in their study that 'what the essay and focus group data suggest is that the exercise of power and authority is a major concern among young people in second level schools'. They found that in schools 'an unrealistic assumption seems to exist about the subordinate status of young persons which is not subjected to serious critical scrutiny' and that young people 'rejected the exercise of traditional authority, the assumption that a teacher was to be obeyed because of the authority vested in his or her role. They sought a greater democratisation of schooling both at the organisational and at the classroom levels'. This research highlights that school decision-making processes are not providing young people with any real experiences of inclusive decision making. Schools are not therefore contributing in any direct way to developing a capacity among young people for the future achievement of political equality objectives in that they continue to employ traditional exclusive forms of decision making within their own structures.

Political equality can be the launching pad for equality in other domains. Zappone highlights that in Ireland and Northern Ireland 'the practices of new forms of governance are creating the political space to reshape the theory and practice of equality'.[44] She refers in Northern Ireland to the requirements in relation to participation by groups experiencing inequality in implementing the statutory duty on the public sector to have due regard to equality. In Ireland she refers to the social partnership model and the participation in this model of social groups experiencing inequality and discrimination.

Cultural Equality

Cultural equality focuses on the issue of difference. Difference in this context includes the identity, experience and situation shared by members of a particular group. Group identity refers to the norms, values and fields of communication or interaction of the group. The relationship and engagement of the group with other dominant groups in society provides the basis for the focus on experience. Economic status, education status, health status or accommodation status makes up the situation of the group. Cultural equality is about the extent to which this difference is acknowledged and valued. It is also about giving practical expression to this valuing of difference in terms of legislation, policy, procedure and practice taking account of any practical implications of such difference. The Task Force on the Travelling community emphasised the importance of this cultural equality in its exploration of institutional discrimination. It highlighted one mechanism by which such discrimination happens: 'Legislation, policy making and provision can be developed without account being taken of their potential impact on a minority cultural group such as the Travellers. In this way policy and practice can develop in a manner that only reflects the "Settled" community's culture and identity and can therefore be inappropriate for the Traveller community.'[45]

Cultural equality is complex. Difference in terms of the identity, experience and situation of a group is not static. It is fluid and subject to constant change as people adapt to new circumstances and contexts. Difference is to be valued and celebrated – but not uncritically. There are dimensions to difference that will disappear in a context of greater equality just as there are elements of difference that will be challenged rather than celebrated in a context of greater equality. One example of where differences should disappear relates to the situation of a group with limited access to income and wealth. In a more equal society income and wealth will be more equally distributed. Those elements of the situation of the group that have been shaped by poverty will inevitably change and disappear in a context of equality.

One example of where difference should be challenged relates to caring roles in the home. There are currently significant gender differences in relation to who plays these caring roles. The accommodation of such differences currently seeks to acknowledge and take into account that these roles are predominantly played by women. This is important in promoting equality for women. However a more equal society should involve a more equal sharing of caring roles between men and women. This difference between women and men in relation to caring roles will therefore diminish in a context of greater equality. It is important that equality strategies, which must currently accommodate this difference, take cognisance of the potential and need for change in how caring roles are shared so as to avoid inadvertently reinforcing inequality in relation to the current imbalance.

Phillips states that she 'cannot see that differences that derive from historical inequalities or relationships of power and subordination can be treated as objects of veneration, differences one would seek to sustain'.[46] She emphasises convergence as one important dimension to equality strategies as a way of addressing these issues in relation to difference. Convergence involves change in the situation, experience and identity of, for example, both men and women so that equality becomes a process of transformation for both groups which could involve new shared traits and practices. This is not a process for all groups or for all differences and she is careful to differentiate it from processes of assimilation. 'Assimilation is certainly no answer, but that is because assimilation is by definition one-way. Convergence, understood as a transformation in the condition of life for both women *and* men, is not objectionable'.

Baker *et al.* address the same concern by promoting the importance of a 'critical interculturalism'.[47] They highlight that 'we show more respect for others by engaging critically with their beliefs than by adopting a *laissez-faire* attitude. The real task is to engage in such criticism in an open and dialogical spirit, recognizing the real effort that the privileged must make to understand the voices of members of subordinate groups and to open their own ideas to critical scrutiny.' The Task Force on the Traveller Community provided an example of this approach of 'critical interculturalism'. Travellers, Traveller organisations and Traveller advocates were in a dialogue with settled people drawn from politics, the statutory sector and the social partners. The starting point for this dialogue was that the distinct Traveller culture and identity should be taken into account. As such the dialogue focused both on change necessary in mainstream institutions to take account of this cultural difference and on what were the key elements of Traveller culture and identity that were appropriate and necessary as a guide to this necessary change. This was an exchange characterised by a 'critical interculturalism'.

Caring equality

Caring equality focuses attention on the experiences of violence, of physical and verbal abuse, of isolation and lack of social contact, of disrespect and of discrimination and exclusion among groups experiencing inequality. Caring equality involves equality in access to relationships of love, care, solidarity or support, respect and trust. This is a relatively underdeveloped focus in debate about effective equality strategies. Caring equality objectives introduce personal relationships and the emotional domain to this debate and subjects these complex and sometimes intangible areas to scrutiny. While these domains might be a relatively new focus, they touch intimately on human worth and have a central contribution to make to quality of life.

This is a focus that has been developed by Baker et al. They reject that these issues could be left aside as private matters. The public sphere can influence and shape the opportunities for emotional development and personal relationships that are available to people and the quality of interaction among people from different groups. They highlight that 'societies can work to establish the condition in which these relationships can thrive'.[48] They suggest that caring equality requires change in 'structures and institutions that systematically impede people's opportunities to develop such relationships including the organisation of paid work, processes of gender stereotyping and the gendered division of labour, attitudes and institutional arrangements concerning disability and, of course, the burden of poverty and deprivation' .

A CONTESTED AMBITION

Equality is a contested concept. There could be a consensus on the rationale for equality. There could be agreement on which groups to focus on in equality strategies. There could be a shared concern at the persistence of inequalities and agreement on the need for change in the economic, political, cultural and caring domains. Yet alongside all this a contest of ideas could coexist – essentially about how far society needs to go or should go in terms of the level of equality sought and in terms of the mechanisms that can be deployed to achieve this level of equality.

This contest of ideas is played out around two poles with positions taken up along the spectrum that exists between them. Liberal egalitarianism can be identified as one pole, and equality of condition can be identified as another pole. It is useful to set out the ideas that relate to each, as it is in this contest of ideas that a societal ambition for equality is defined.

Liberal egalitarianism is a field of analysis that encompasses a wide range of views. However, a number of key characteristics can be identified. Baker *et al.* identify a key assumption that underpins this ambition for equality as being 'that there will always be major inequalities between people in their status, resources, work and power. The role of the ideal of equality is to provide a fair basis for managing these inequalities, by strengthening the minimum to which everyone is entitled and by using equality of opportunity to regulate the competition for advantage.'[49]

Those who espouse liberal egalitarianism emphasise non-discrimination and equality of opportunity. They prioritise a focus on the individual rather than examining disparities between groups. They focus on citizenship and on equality in people's status as citizens and on the rights and responsibilities that flow from being citizens. They promote tolerance as a response to difference. They restrict their attention to the public realm deeming significant areas to be of private concern and therefore beyond the reach of equality strategies.

The central problem with this liberal egalitarianism is that it can accept and coexist with significant levels of inequality. It is a significant influence on the current strategic framework for action on equality in Ireland as is evidenced by the emphasis on anti-discrimination and equality of opportunity. Yet, as outlined earlier in this chapter, significant inequalities persist in the Irish context. There is a further problem in that the commitment to liberal egalitarianism can mask or even justify this persistent inequality. Under cover of a supposed fairness and an apparent right for individuals to make their own choices, a consensus is affirmed that there is little more that can be done to improve the way society is organised, structured and managed – yet inequality persists. Liberal egalitarian strategies therefore end up being 'about regulating inequality rather than eliminating it'.[50]

There is also a double-edged nature to some of the core concepts deployed by those who espouse this liberal egalitarianism. Tolerance is emphasised as a key dimension to the management of diversity in society. Yet as Phillips points out 'tolerance of this sort can easily coexist with ignorance and can certainly coexist with contempt. Those who have agreed to tolerate may feel themselves absolved from any further moves towards better understanding; and since majority groups rarely conceive of themselves as requiring equal doses of tolerance from the minority, they may come to wear their toleration as an additional badge of superiority.'[51]

The search to go beyond liberal egalitarianism is often met with the critique that going further is about the imposition of sameness, of rigid structures and ways of doing things or of some sort of mathematical equality. To go beyond liberal egalitarianism is not about enforcing sameness. It is about ensuring meaningful choices. To go beyond liberal egalitarianism is about the removal of rigid structures and hierarchies that confine groups to the periphery from one generation to the next. To go beyond liberal egalitarianism is not about a mathematical equality but is certainly about making significant inroads into current levels of inequality. Phillips highlights that 'the idea that equality depends on everyone being the same can also be regarded as an unequitable assimilationism that imposes the values and norms of one group on those who were historically subordinate',[52] and that 'egalitarians do not (cannot) think that people have to be made equal in every respect' and that 'we cannot hope to eliminate all differences in economic circumstances. We can, more plausibly, hope to abolish those permanent hierarchies that put people for life into one kind of group.'

The opposing pole to liberal egalitarianism is equality of condition. This involves a far greater ambition for equality.

Baker et al describe it in terms of aiming 'to eliminate major inequalities altogether, or at least massively to reduce the current scale of inequality'.[53] This therefore moves beyond the management and regulation of inequality to strategies that seek to eliminate inequality.

Those who espouse equality of condition emphasise the role of structures and systems in a society characterised by significant inequalities. These structures and systems encompass how all the different element of society are organised – the economic, cultural, political and social elements. Those who espouse equality of condition seek to focus on root causes and to identify how inequalities are generated and passed on from generation to generation by these structures and systems. They promote the need to review how we manage and organise society and to develop alternative structures and systems that can break cycles of inequality, that can redress legacies of inequality and that can realise a sense of belonging and ownership for all. They are concerned with choice rather than sameness. Equality of condition is about 'enabling and empowering people to make real choices among real options'.[54] Those who espouse equality of condition move beyond tolerance of difference to the celebration of difference, they accord value to diversity and seek an accommodation of the practical implication of difference and diversity. They bring a broad focus to needs that go beyond income and wealth to include access to the wider range of resources necessary for people to realise their choices. They break with traditional understandings of private and public realms to seek a coherent contribution in all areas to eliminating inequality.

CONCLUSION

This brief exploration of equality and a vision for a more equal society provides a starting point for an exploration of the more practical dimensions to promoting equality and combating discrimination. The dominant understanding of and vision for equality will shape each dimension to the framework for action and will inevitably define the extent to which it can realise a more equal society.

The strategic framework for action on equality needs to go beyond liberal concepts of equality and seek substantive change in current inequalities. In this it needs to embrace the ambition that informs the goal of equality of condition.

The strategic framework needs to be comprehensive in its approach to equality. The current equality legislation provides a valuable starting point in this regard with its coverage of nine different grounds. These grounds encompass a broad range of groups that experience inequality and bring forward a range of common themes that need to be a focus for equality objectives established within the strategic framework. There remain gaps in this approach in that it does not cover all grounds experiencing inequality including the significant absence of a socio-economic status ground.

Finally the strategic framework needs to have a capacity to take action to support equality across a broad range of objectives. These include economic equality, political equality, cultural equality and caring equality.

The following chapters explore the key dimensions to the strategic framework – institutions, legislation, mainstreaming and targeting. They set out the mechanisms that have been put in place under each dimension to promote equality and combat discrimination. They identify issues that have been raised in implementing these mechanisms. Finally they look to the further development of these mechanisms and dimensions so that they more effectively contribute to an equality of condition for all groups experiencing inequality.

NOTES

1. *A Strategic Policy Framework for Equality Issues*, National Economic and Social Forum (Dublin) 2002
2. Baker, J., Lynch, K., Cantillon, S. and Walsh, J., *Equality From Theory to Action*, Palgrave Macmillan (Hampshire) 2004
3. Phillips, A., *Which Equalities Matter*, Polity Press (Cambridge) 1999
4. Zappone, K., *Charting the Equality Agenda: A Coherent Framework for Equality Strategies in Ireland North and South*, Equality Authority and Equality Commission for Northern Ireland (Dublin) 2001
5. *Communiqué – Towards More and Better Jobs* – Meeting of Employment and Labour Ministers, 29–30 September, 2003, Paris OECD, 2003
6. *On Guidelines for the Employment Policies of Member States*, EU Council Decision, 22 July 2003
7. Phillips, A., *Which Equalities Matter*, Polity Press (Cambridge) 1999
8. *Women and Men in Ireland 2004*, Central Statistics Office, Stationary Office (Dublin) 2004
9. Gannon and Nolan, *Disability and Labour Market Participation*, Equality Authority (Dublin) 2004
10. Conroy, P. and Brennan A., *Migrant Workers and their Experiences*, Equality Authority (Dublin) 2003
11. *Accommodating Diversity in Labour Market Programmes*, WRC Social & Economic Consultants, Equality Authority (Dublin) 2003
12. *Accommodating Diversity in Labour Market Programmes*, WRC Social & Economic Consultants, Equality Authority (Dublin) 2003
13. Cullen, Delaney, Duff, *Caring Working and Public Policy*, Equality Authority (Dublin) 2004
14. Lodge A. and Lynch K., (eds), *Diversity at School*, Equality Authority (Dublin) 2005
15. *Accommodating Diversity in Labour Market Programmes*, Lodge A. and Lynch K., (eds), *Accommodating Diversity in Labour Market Programmes*, WRC Social & Economic Consultants, Equality Authority (Dublin) 2003
16. Lodge A. and Lynch K., (eds), *Diversity at School*, Equality Authority (Dublin) 2005
17. Lodge A. and Lynch K., (eds), *Diversity at School*, Equality Authority (Dublin) 2005
18. *Women and Men in Ireland 2004*, Central Statistics Office, Stationary Office (Dublin) 2004
19. *Poverty and Inequality – Applying an Equality Dimension to Poverty Proofing*, Equality Authority and Combat Poverty Agency (Dublin) 2003
20. *Poverty and Inequality – Applying an Equality Dimension to Poverty Proofing*, Equality Authority and Combat Poverty Agency (Dublin) 2003
21. Collins, E. and Sheehan, B., *Access to Health Services for Transsexual People*, Equality Authority (Dublin) 2004
22. *Annual Count Figures 2003*, Department of Environment, Heritage and Local Government (Dublin) 2003

23. *Poverty and Inequality – Applying an Equality Dimension to Poverty Proofing*, Equality Authority and Combat Poverty Agency (Dublin) 2003

24. *Poverty and Inequality – Applying an Equality Dimension to Poverty Proofing*, Equality Authority and Combat Poverty Agency (Dublin) 2003

25. *Women and Men in Ireland 2004*, Central Statistics Office, Stationary Office (Dublin) 2004

26. *Women and Men in Ireland 2004*, Central Statistics Office, Stationary Office (Dublin) 2004

27. *Implementing Equality for Lesbians Gays and Bisexuals*, Equality Authority (Dublin) 2002

28. Lynch, K. and Lodge, A., *Equality and Power in Schools – Redistribution, Recognition and Representation*, Routledge Falmer (London) 2002

29. Collins, E. and Sheehan, B., *Access to Health Services for Transsexual People*, Equality Authority (Dublin) 2004

30. *Report of the Task Force on the Travelling Community*, Stationery Office (Dublin) 1995

31. *Poverty and Inequality – Applying an Equality Dimension to Poverty Proofing*, Equality Authority and Combat Poverty Agency (Dublin) 2003

32. Nexus Research Cooperative, *Singular Responses – Working for Change*, Dingle Peninsula Men's Action Group

33. *Implementing Equality for Carers*, Equality Authority, to be published 2005

34. *Women and Men in Ireland 2004*, Central Statistics Office, Stationary Office (Dublin) 2004

35. *Report for the Working Group on the Review of the Parental Leave Act 1998*, Department of Justice, Equality and Law Reform (Dublin) 2002.

36. Phillips, A., *Which Equalities Matter*, Polity Press (Cambridge) 1999

37. 2. Baker, J., Lynch, K., Cantillon, S. and Walsh, J., *Equality From Theory to Action*, Palgrave Macmillan (Hampshire) 2004

38. Zappone, K., *Charting the Equality Agenda: A Coherent Framework for Equality Strategies in Ireland North and South*, Equality Authority and Equality Commission for Northern Ireland (Dublin) 2001

39. Phillips, A., *Which Equalities Matter*, Polity Press (Cambridge) 1999

40. Baker, J., Lynch, K., Cantillon, S. and Walsh, J., *Equality From Theory to Action*, Palgrave Macmillan (Hampshire) 2004

41. Phillips, A., *Which Equalities Matter*, Polity Press (Cambridge) 1999

42. Baker, J., Lynch, K., Cantillon, S. and Walsh, J., *Equality From Theory to Action*, Palgrave Macmillan (Hampshire) 2004

43. Lynch, K. and Lodge, A., *Equality and Power in Schools – Redistribution, Recognition and Representation*, Routledge Falmer (London) 2002

44. Zappone, K., *Charting the Equality Agenda: A Coherent Framework for Equality Strategies in Ireland North and South*, Equality Authority and Equality Commission for Northern Ireland (Dublin) 2001

45. *Poverty and Inequality – Applying an Equality Dimension to Poverty Proofing*, Equality Authority and Combat Poverty Agency (Dublin) 2003

46. Phillips, A., *Which Equalities Matter*, Polity Press (Cambridge) 1999

47. Baker, J., Lynch, K., Cantillon, S. and Walsh, J., *Equality From Theory to*

Action, Palgrave Macmillan (Hampshire) 2004

48. Baker, J., Lynch, K., Cantillon, S. and Walsh, J., *Equality From Theory to Action*, Palgrave Macmillan (Hampshire) 2004

49. Baker, J., Lynch, K., Cantillon, S. and Walsh, J., *Equality From Theory to Action*, Palgrave Macmillan (Hampshire) 2004

50. Baker, J., Lynch, K., Cantillon, S. and Walsh, J., *Equality From Theory to Action*, Palgrave Macmillan (Hampshire) 2004

51. Phillips, A., *Which Equalities Matter*, Polity Press (Cambridge) 1999

52. Phillips, A., *Which Equalities Matter*, Polity Press (Cambridge) 1999

53. Baker, J., Lynch, K., Cantillon, S. and Walsh, J., *Equality From Theory to Action*, Palgrave Macmillan (Hampshire) 2004

54. Baker, J., Lynch, K., Cantillon, S. and Walsh, J., *Equality From Theory to Action*, Palgrave Macmillan (Hampshire) 2004

Chapter Two

Institutions Promoting Equality

The Annual Report of an institution provides a record of its work during the previous year. It is an important moment to take stock of progress made and to highlight trends. A quick track back through the media headlines for Equality Authority Annual Reports provides a flavour of the breadth of its mandate and work.

'No Clean Slate for State on Prejudice' was the *Irish Independent* headline of 20th May 2004. The Equality Authority Annual Report 2003 stated that 'a substantial number of Equality Authority case files under the Equal Status Act concern allegations of discrimination across a wide range of grounds against public bodies' and highlighted 'the need for public bodies to equality proof their policies, practices and procedures to assess their impact across the nine grounds and to ensure they contribute to equality and do not discriminate'.[1]

The *Irish Examiner* headline of 6th March 2003 ran 'Pregnant Women Still Being Sacked Warns Authority'. The 2002 Annual Report stated that 'The Labour Court is sending out a strong unequivocal message that discrimination against pregnant women will not be tolerated and employers who discriminate will have to pay substantial financial compensation. This meaningful remedy should serve as a real deterrent to this type of discrimination.'[2]

'Travellers Turn to Equality Authority' was the *Sunday*

Business Post headline on 30th June 2002. The Annual Report for 2001 had identified that under the Equal Status Act the 'overwhelming volume of cases arising was unexpected and unprecedented particularly in the area of refusal of service by publicans to members of the Traveller community' and that this was indicative of 'persistent, sustained and endemic discrimination and a profound reluctance to make this arena of social interaction more inclusive'.[3]

The first Annual Report of the Equality Authority covered the year 2000. This had noted that 'the challenge is to ensure that compensation awards are effective, proportionate and dissuasive on all of the nine grounds'.[4] The *Irish Independent* headline for 3rd July 2001 emphasised this, stating '£50,000 Award to Doctor "a Sea Change in Equality Cases"'.

The Equality Authority lies at the heart of the strategic framework for action on equality. This is because its functions are established in the Employment Equality Acts and the Equal Status Acts which make up the core legislative dimension to the strategic framework. These functions include a dual mandate to both promote equality of opportunity and to combat discrimination in the areas covered by the legislation. This dual mandate involves the Equality Authority in playing enforcement and developmental roles that reflect both the obligations provided for in the legislation and the ambitions for equality that led to the enactment of the legislation. The Equality Authority is accorded an information function on the equality legislation and on maternity protection, adoptive leave and parental leave legislation. This function involves the Equality Authority in playing a range of communication roles. Another important function of the Equality Authority is to keep the implementation of the equality legislation under review and to make recommendations for change in this legislation as necessary.

The Equality Authority exercises its mandate in a context where there are other institutions that play roles within the strategic framework for action on equality. These institutions also derive their mandates from legislation. They include the Irish Human Rights Commission, the National Council on Ageing and Older People, the National Disability Authority and the Combat Poverty Agency. There is also the non-statutory National Consultative Committee on Racism and Interculturalism. There is a challenge in this context to ensure that the mandate of the Equality Authority is exercised in a manner that is integrated and coherent with the wide range of institutions playing roles within the strategic framework for action on equality.

Within this strategic framework these institutions can play roles in sustaining, evolving, linking and operating the other core dimensions of the framework – legislation, mainstreaming, targeting, participation, agenda setting, and monitoring and review. These institutions can play roles in maintaining a focus on equality and developing new knowledge, analysis and understanding of equality issues and of strategies to achieve equality. They can play roles in driving forward change for greater equality and supporting all other organisations and institutions to make their contribution to equality as employers and service providers and within other roles that these organisations and institutions play.

This chapter seeks to illustrate the institutional dimension to the strategic framework through an exploration of the work of the Equality Authority. The Equality Authority is chosen not only because it is established under the equality legislation but also because of its broad mandate. This covers the nine grounds of gender, marital status, family status, age, disability, sexual orientation, race, religion and membership of the Traveller community. It includes a focus on the workplace and on the provision of goods and services, accommodation and educational establishments.

The work of the Equality Authority is explored under the headings of integration, of change and of future perspectives. The theme of integration is explored in terms of how the Equality Authority implements the multi-ground nature of its mandate and how it seeks a coherence and integration with the work of other statutory institutions within this strategic framework for action on equality. The theme of change is examined in terms of the different ways in which the Equality Authority works to promote equality and to achieve the change necessary to realise equality objectives. This work is explored under the headings of enforcement for change, negotiation for change, cultural action for change and knowledge development for change. Finally, the theme of future perspectives is analysed to identify how the Equality Authority should be further developed as part of the growth and development of the strategic framework for action on equality.

INTEGRATION – A MULTI-GROUND AGENDA

In 2002 the Equality Authority and the Equality Commission for Northern Ireland published a report by Katherine Zappone entitled *Charting the Equality Agenda – a Coherent Framework for Equality Strategies in Ireland North and South*. The study sought to explore integrated approaches to equality that cover a broad range of grounds and to identify strategies for putting such an approach into effect.

> Considerable inequality and discrimination exist in both the Republic of Ireland and Northern Ireland. The material resources, political power, meaning and relationships – or the economic, political, cultural and social structures – are organised in such a way that many groups and individuals are inhibited in their capacity for self determination and to fully participate in society. Imagine bringing together these diverse perspectives and experiences in some integrative fashion. The process and outcomes of such an approach could hold the potential to effect a radical change dynamic, namely to reorganise structures so that conditions are created for the flourishing of diverse ways of being human.[5]

She found that integrated approaches to equality provide 'the opportunity to redefine a positive and substantive meaning of equality, as one that includes the diversity of background and aspiration of all members of society' and that they hold 'the potential to increase the effectiveness and efficiency of equality work'. Integrated approaches to equality, she suggested, 'necessarily progress the democratisation of society and the economy'.

The Equality Authority and the Equality Commission for Northern Ireland had found themselves facing broadly similar challenges. Both jurisdictions had developed an approach to equality that had moved away from fragmented approaches to equality tied to the specific identity, experience and situation of individual groups. Both institutions were in the unique situation of working to combat discrimination and promote equality across a multi-ground agenda that sought to be comprehensive by covering a broad range of groups experiencing inequality.

This joint report on the value in and the practice of an integrated approach to a multi-ground equality agenda suggested the need for the two institutions to work at three different levels – a multi-ground level, a single ground level and a cross-ground level.

Initiatives that have a multi-ground focus are central to integrated approaches to equality. Such initiatives focus on all nine grounds covered by the equality legislation. They establish the connections between these grounds and are developed to enhance the experience and situation of people across all nine grounds.

Much of the core developmental work of the Equality Authority reflects this multi-ground approach. Initiatives to support an equality dimension to quality customer service in the public sector have emphasised the need to include the nine grounds covered by the equality legislation. Employers have been resourced and supported to review their employment policies, practices and procedures for their impact on equality in the workplace through a scheme of Employment Equality Reviews and Action Plans that encompasses all nine grounds. Initiatives to support inclusive schools and equality competent health service organisations are based on the needs of all nine grounds. It is also of interest to note the growth in casework supported by the Equality Authority of cases where claimants allege discrimination on more than one ground. In 2004 these accounted for 8.2% of all case files whereas in 2001 they accounted for 4.2% of all case files.

Initiatives that focus on a single ground have a relevance within integrated approaches to equality. They form part of an integrated approach because despite their focus on a single ground, the institution that is bringing the initiative forward has a multi-ground remit and develops and implements the initiative out of a consciousness, commitment and practice that has a multi-ground focus. Single ground initiatives are important where there is a risk that the ground could become invisible within multi-ground initiatives. They are necessary where people within a single ground have needs that are specific to that ground. They are valuable where particular opportunities become available to enhance the situation or experience of people within a single ground.

The Equality Authority committed to develop new initiatives specific to the gender ground in its 2005 business plan. The Central Statistics Office had just produced a report *Women and Men in Ireland 2004.*[6] This identified the persistence of significant inequalities for women. The Department of Justice, Equality and Law Reform signalled its intent to produce a National Strategy for Women during 2005. This was on foot of commitments made to the United Nations in relation to the Beijing Conference on Gender Equality and in the Sustaining Progress national agreement. The proposed National Strategy for Women presented a particular opportunity to advance gender equality and the report of the Central Statistics Office provided a particular stimulus to prioritise this focus. Both provided the rationale for new gender-specific initiatives by the Equality Authority.

Integrated approaches to equality include a cross-ground level of work. The starting point for this level of work is that people can be members of more than one ground. A cross-ground level of work involves a focus on the multiple identities people hold – as Travellers with disabilities, as older gay men or as minority ethnic women, for example. People who hold multiple identities present a new range of identities, experiences and situations that have not been adequately included in equality strategies that have been specific to a single ground. They are distinct identities, experiences and situations in that by combining differences unique experiences emerge that shape new norms and values and contribute to new situations for these groups.

'Re-Thinking Identity' is a research project developed by the Joint Equality and Human Rights Forum in 2003. The Forum involves the Equality Authority, the Irish Human Rights Commission, the Equality Commission for Northern Ireland, the Northern Ireland Human Rights Commission, the Disability Rights Commission (GB), the Equal Opportunities Commission (GB) and the Commission for Racial Equality (GB). The project was developed to give visibility to particular multiple identity groups. Separate initiatives explored the identity, experience and situation of disabled minority ethnic people, Black and minority ethnic women, disabled gay and lesbian people, disabled women, young lesbian and gay people and young minority ethnic men.

Katherine Zappone, who edited the research report, stated in her conclusion that the research 'depicts how people's identities are multiple, changing and at times imbued with contradictions. The studies document that people who hold multiple identities experience acute prejudicial attitudes and disrespect'. She highlighted that the research findings 'offer a new platform from which to think about the core principle of "diversity" in the work of equality and human rights bodies'.[7]

The Equality Authority commissioned the research initiative on disabled minority ethnic people. Maria Pierce, who carried out this research, concluded that 'Disabled, minority, ethnic people face discrimination not only on the basis of disability but also racist discrimination. They can face barriers preventing them from integrating into Irish society such as lack of access to social networks or language and cultural differences. They occupy a minority position within the disability sector as well as within organisations and groups representing minority ethnic groups.'[8]

There are potential pitfalls that need to be addressed with the integrated approach to promoting equality. It is necessary to monitor the visibility afforded to each ground so that particular groups are not omitted from the integrated approach. Diversity needs to remain central to the intergrated approach. The multi-ground level of work within the integrated approach must not homogenise the various groups in seeking to promote equality for a broad range of groups. The specific identity, experience and situation of each group will continue to have its own particular practical implications even within a context where elements of difference are shared across the various groups.

The integrated approach to equality, however, has significant potential. This potential lies in:

- the administrative simplicity allowed by the integrated approach to equality. Organiszations can develop a single strategy to combat discrimination and to promote equality of opportunity. This is significantly easier to implement than a requirement to develop and pursue nine separate strategies;

- the solidarity an integrated approach can engender between the different grounds. This is a solidarity that groups within the grounds need to build and sustain. These different groups can identify shared needs and aspirations and develop a consensus among themselves as to priorities to be pursued together within an integrated approach to equality. This is a solidarity that involves a broad and powerful constituency for change by bringing such a broad range of groups together to work towards shared equality objectives;

- the limiting of hierarchies between different groups and different forms of discrimination within an integrated approach. An integrated approach to equality can be comprehensive in including all groups that experience inequality given the administrative simplicity it allows. The alternative to an integrated approach involves choices being made that prioritise particular grounds at the expense of others. If each new group identified as experiencing inequality and discrimination requires its own legislation, institutions and mainstreaming strategies, progress on equality will remain slow and exclusive to some groups;

- the inclusion of multiple identity groups within an integrated approach, such as gay and lesbian Travellers, older women and young people with disabilities, for example. These multiple identity groups bring their own diversity that needs to be valued and to be taken into account in policies, programmes and practices;

- the learning that can accumulate as each group within the integrated approach shares its history and strategies. Traveller groups have made identity a central issue in their strategies for equality. People with disabilities have brought forward the issue of a disabling society and the importance of making reasonable accommodations or adjustments for people with disabilities. Family friendly working arrangements have been a key focus in strategies for gender equality. These concepts of identity, reasonable accommodation and flexible working arrangements – and there are others deployed by other groups – have been taken up and applied in equality strategies by other groups experiencing inequality. Making links between groups experiencing inequality can generate a creativity that enhances the effectiveness of the equality strategies for all groups.

INTEGRATION – INSTITUTIONAL COHERENCE

In recent times there has been an impressive development of statutory institutions whose roles and areas of work involve making a contribution to the promotion of equality. The establishment of the Equality Authority has been followed by the establishment of the National Disability Authority and the Irish Human Rights Commission. It was preceded by the establishment of the Combat Poverty Agency and the National Council on Ageing and Older People. There is also the National Consultative Committee on Racism and Interculturalism.

The Human Rights Commission Act 2000 made provision for the setting up of the Irish Human Rights Commission. The mandate of the Commission is to promote and protect people's human rights as guaranteed to them by the Constitution and by international agreements to which the State is a party. The National Disability Authority was established on foot of the National Disability Authority Act 1999. The principal function of the National Disability Authority is to advise the Minister for Justice, Equality and Law Reform and keep him or her informed of developments in relation to people with disabilities which concern issues of policy and practice. The National Council on Ageing and Older People was established by statutory instrument in March 1997 to advise the Minister for Health and Children on all aspects of ageing and the welfare of older people. The Combat Poverty Agency is the statutory body established to advise the government on economic and social issues relating to poverty through research, project innovation and evaluation and public education. The National Consultative Committee on Racism and Interculturalism was established in 1998 as an independent expert body focusing on racism and interculturalism. It is not a statutory institution but a partnership organisation that brings together governmental and non-governmental organisations to develop an inclusive and strategic approach to combating racism by focusing on the prevention of racism and on promoting an intercultural society.

The work of this array of institutions needs to be coherent and integrated if the strategic framework for action on equality is to be effectively deployed in pursuit of equality objectives. Coherence and integration means:

- the avoidance of duplication in the initiatives of the various institutions;
- the identification and addressing of any gaps in the provision of the various institutions and in their response to the different groups experiencing inequality;
- the development of a shared understanding of equality objectives, issues of inequality and strategies for equality;
- the implementation of joint ventures on issues of shared concern;
- the creation of joint planning processes that make links between the work and initiatives of the various institutions.

The Irish Human Rights Commission and the Equality Authority have sought a coherence and integration in their work through a Memorandum of Understanding between the two organisations. This emphasises the independence and distinct mandate of each organisation but commits to:

- consultation with one another in drafting respective strategic plans and business plans;
- consultation with one another in developing and reviewing criteria for casework and wider strategic enforcement strategies;
- identification of matters for joint action and for linked and mutually supportive actions;
- sharing expertise and learning and encouraging interaction between staff.

An island of Ireland dimension to this search for coherence and integration in the work of institutions with a remit in relation to equality is also evident in the cooperation developed between the Equality Authority and the Equality Commission for Northern Ireland. The Equality Commission for Northern Ireland was established in 1999. It incorporated the functions of the Fair Employment Commission for Northern Ireland, the Equal Opportunities Commission for Northern Ireland, the Commission for Racial Equality for Northern Ireland and the Northern Ireland Disability Council. It also has powers and function in relation to the equality duties imposed on public authorities by the Northern Ireland Act 1998.

Cooperation between organisations in different jurisdictions can be developed at different levels of ambition. Three such levels of ambition in cooperation can be identified – ad hoc, instrumental and strategic. The most basic level of ambition is ad hoc cooperation. This is limited to meetings or exchanges between personnel in organisations. At a more advanced level of ambition is instrumental cooperation. This involves organisations working together for a common purpose. However, this is project based and largely shaped by available funding and it remains short term. At a more ambitious level of cooperation is strategic cooperation. Organisations involved in strategic cooperation share a vision in terms of what is to be achieved and have common long-term objectives in relation to this vision. They identify a common purpose and develop mutually agreed agendas to progress this common purpose.

The Equality Authority and the Equality Commission for Northern Ireland have sought to develop a cooperation that is strategic. They have worked to develop a shared vision through the joint research project 'Charting the Equality Agenda – A Coherent Framework for Equality Strategies in Ireland, North and South'. This explored:

- the vision for equality the two organisations might seek to pursue;
- the methodologies and approaches that could be deployed by both organisations to manage a multi-ground equality agenda.

The strategic ambition of this cooperation is further reflected in structures. A joint Board meeting is held on an annual basis. This explores equality issues and strategies of shared concern and initiates a series of joint ventures.

The cooperation between the Equality Authority and the Equality Commission for Northern Ireland has also involved an East-West dimension as both organisations participate in the Joint Equality and Human Rights Forum. This brings together the equality and human rights bodies in Ireland, Northern Ireland and Britain. The forum meets annually and has defined its role in terms of providing a forum for the exchange of information and experience, promoting partnership working between the organisations and communicating equality and human rights best practice.

EQUALITY AUTHORITY – POWERS AND MISSION

The Equality Authority set out its understanding of equality in its Strategic Plan 2003–05. This is an understanding of equality that has economic, political, cultural and caring objectives which address:

- Redistribution, involving access to resources and economic activity;
- Representation, involving access to decision-making and a capacity to organise;
- Recognition, involving an acknowledgement and a valuing of the different identities, experiences and situations of the groups experiencing inequality;
- Respect, involving an underpinning of the inter-dependence and mutual support aspects of human welfare.[9]

The Equality Authority has been given a range of powers to implement its mandate to promote equality of opportunity and to combat discrimination in the areas covered by the Employment Equality Acts and the Equal Status Act. The Equality Authority has powers to support an individual enforcement of the legislation. Individual enforcement involves an individual who alleges discrimination seeking redress under the legislation. The Equality Authority is also afforded powers that go beyond this individual enforcement. The Equality Authority can deploy these powers to seek change in institutional practices and to promote equality not just for the individual but for groups that experience inequality.

At the level of individual enforcement a person who considers that they have been discriminated against can apply to the Equality Authority for assistance in bringing a case under the equality legislation. The Equality Authority has a broad discretion to grant assistance if it is satisfied that the case raises an important point of principle or if it appears to the Equality Authority that it is not reasonable to expect the person to adequately present the case without assistance. This involves the Equality Authority in work of strategic litigation rather than the provision of a broad legal service for all. Strategic litigation involves choosing cases on the basis of criteria established by the Equality Authority. These criteria focus on cases most likely to have a ripple effect, to create legal precedent or to further equality objectives established by the Equality Authority.

The Equality Authority has a number of powers that allow it to combat discrimination and promote equality in a manner that addresses institutional practice and the experience and situation of groups that experience inequality. These include codes of practice, equality reviews and inquiries. The Equality Authority can prepare Codes of Practice to further the elimination of discrimination or the promotion of equality in the areas covered by the legislation. Such codes of practice are, if approved by the Minister for Justice, Equality and Law Reform, admissible in evidence and if relevant may be taken into account in proceedings under the legislation. The Equality Authority has produced a code of practice on Sexual Harassment and Harassment at Work. The aim of the code is to give 'practical guidance to employers, employer organisations, trade unions and employees on:

- what is meant by sexual harassment and harassment in the workplace;
- how it may be prevented;
- what steps to take if it does occur to ensure that adequate procedures are readily available to deal with the problem and to prevent its recurrence.[10]

The Equality Authority can invite an organisation to carry out an equality review and to prepare and implement an equality action plan. It can carry out such a review and prepare an action plan on its own initiative where appropriate and where the organisation under review does not have less than fifty employees. An equality review is an audit of the level of equality of opportunity in the organisation and an examination of policies, practices and procedures in the organisation to determine whether these contribute to the promotion of equality of opportunity. An equality action plan is a programme of actions to further the promotion of equality of opportunity in the organisation. There are enforcement powers in respect of equality reviews and action plans. This power has been described as having 'great potential as a non adversarial fault finding mechanism which moves beyond the individual enforcement model'.[11]

The Equality Authority has a broad power to conduct an inquiry for any purpose connected with its functions. It can make recommendations arising out of the inquiry and may issue non-discrimination notices. This has been described as 'a particularly useful power in situations where potential claimants may be very vulnerable or where there is a dearth of information'.[12]

Since its establishment the Equality Authority has worked to a mission statement that reflects a commitment to change for individuals experiencing discrimination, to change in institutional practices and to societal change. This mission statement is set out as:

'The Equality Authority is committed to realising positive change in the situation of those experiencing inequality by:

1. promoting and defending the rights established in the equality legislation; and
2. providing leadership in:
   • building a commitment to addressing equality issues in practice.
   • creating a wider awareness of equality issues.
   • celebrating the diversity in Irish society.
   • mainstreaming equality considerations across all sectors.'[13]

The first strategic plan of the Equality Authority established a range of core values that would inform its work. Independence is one such value. The strategic plan states that 'we have responsibilities to a wide range of diverse constituencies. We will realise those responsibilities with integrity and in a balanced and coherent manner that reflects the independence of our position'. Partnership is another core value with the strategic plan stating: 'Our work will be based on a participative approach. Our working relations with equality organisations, the four pillars of social partnership, the public sector and those who avail themselves of our services will be characterised by partnership.' Solidarity is identified as a core value where the strategic plan states: 'Our pursuit of equality acknowledges the importance of those groups experiencing inequality determining their own agenda for change. We aim to enhance the voice of such groups in articulating and progressing their agendas.'[14]

The Equality Authority pursued a broad approach to its mandate in its first strategic plan. This allowed for a flexibility that enabled a new institution that was breaking new ground to test out a variety of approaches and to seek out those areas where progress could be made. The Equality Authority was breaking new ground in that its mandate covered both employment and the provision of goods and services accommodation and educational establishments and in that it was committed to developing an integrated approach to equality across the nine different grounds. The Equality Authority planned for this flexibility by organising its work behind three broad objectives.

The first objective was to 'promote and defend the rights established under the Employment Equality Act 1998 and the Equal Status legislation, when enacted'.[15] Initiatives under this objective involved communication work to build a consciousness of the rights established. A strategic approach to casework under the legislation was undertaken and research that would underpin and reinforce casework activity was commissioned.

'We will support the development of a capacity to realise equality outcomes in the workplace and in the provision of goods, facilities, services, education and accommodation'[16] was the second objective. Initiatives under this objective involved providing guidance and direction on effective equality strategies alongside the development of demonstration projects. Research work was carried out to generate new commitments to and new thinking about achieving equality outcomes, alongside initiatives to support the gathering of data and the development of indicators to measure progress towards greater equality.

The final objective was to 'contribute to a mainstreaming of equality within the private and public sectors and a focus on equality issues across society'.[17] Initiatives under this objective involved developing a programme of voluntary employment equality reviews and action plans and resourcing and stimulating a focus on equality in a range of policy-making areas. Work was carried out to contribute to building a culture of equality in Irish society.

The Equality Authority sought to concentrate its resources in a defined number of key areas in its second strategic plan. This is reflected in the commitment to 'prioritising particular issues and areas of life and focusing our work on achieving progress in these'.[18] This commitment is pursued through six themes, which served to direct and integrate the different functions, powers and resources of the Equality Authority.

The first theme was to build 'equality in service provision that impacts on the quality of people's lives'. This involved the Equality Authority in work in the fields of education and health and within the Quality Customer Service initiative of the public sector. 'Contributing to a more accessible workplace and labour market' was the second theme. The Equality Authority sought to balance its work on the areas covered by the Employment Equality Acts and on the areas covered by the Equal Status Acts with these two themes. The work under these two themes was principally developed on a multi-ground level.

The Equality Authority identified the need to work at a single ground level in the third theme. This theme was 'developing initiatives specific to the disability ground, to the issue of racism and the issues of carers under the family status ground'. The disability ground was chosen because of the specific provision on reasonable accommodation of people with disabilities in the equality legislation. The issue of racism was chosen because of the growing virulence and visibility of racism in Irish society. The issue of carers was chosen to support a visibility for carers within integrated multi-ground approaches to equality.

The fourth theme identified the Equality Authority's commitment to reinforcing and developing the wider strategic framework for action on equality within which it operates. This theme was 'supporting the development of effective equality strategies at national and local levels'. Work under this theme involved initiatives to support the further development of equality legislation, of equality and diversity training, of equality proofing and of equality data. This work also contributed to the development of a local equality infrastructure – to creating local strategic frameworks for action on equality to match that which is being developed at national level.

The fifth theme was to address 'the specific situation and experience of those within the nine grounds faced with additional barriers of poverty and exclusion'. Initiatives in this area sought to enable those responsible for anti-poverty policies and programmes to take account of diversity across the nine grounds among people living in poverty. The interface between the experiences of inequality and poverty was the focus for this theme. The final theme was 'maintaining and developing the internal structures and systems of the Equality Authority'.

The work of the Equality Authority is now explored across four different strands of work. These strands identify the different ways in which the Equality Authority has sought to contribute to change for individuals, institutions and society. The change sought by the Equality Authority through these different strands is the change necessary for the achievement of equality objectives of redistribution, representation, recognition and respect.[19] The four strands of work are:

- enforcement for change;
- negotiation for change;
- cultural action for change;
- knowledge development for change.

EQUALITY AUTHORITY – ENFORCEMENT FOR CHANGE

Three cases illustrate what enforcement for change is about and the potential impact this strand of activity can hold. The cases described involve the Equal Status Acts and the Employment Equality Acts. The cases involve the disability ground, the race ground and the gender ground.

In early 2004 Para Equestrian Ireland was found by the Circuit Court to have victimised a visually impaired rider under the provisions of the Equal Status Act. Para Equestrian Ireland is a voluntary sector organisation providing a support service to people with disabilities competing in dressage events. Joan Salmon who took the case is a visually impaired rider with significant achievements in the sport. The Equality Authority provided her with legal representation. The Circuit Court ordered Para Equestrian Ireland to re-admit Joan Salmon to full membership of and participation in the sporting events of the association and to provide her with reasonable accommodation to allow her to participate fully and awarded her €3,500.

The case arose from the organisation's refusal to allow her to bring her guide dog with her to an equestrian event in Scotland in June 2001. At first she was told that the refusal was due to foot and mouth restrictions in Scotland. However she claimed that the Department of Agriculture and the Gleneagles Equestrian Centre told her that there was no such problem. Para Equestrian Ireland then told her it would create too much work if she were to bring the guide dog. The issue was raised in the media and Joan Salmon was then refused entry to all future events under the control of Para Equestrian Ireland until she gave a written apology for comments made in the media. She made an apology but it was not accepted because it was deemed inadequate. During this time Joan Salmon missed out on the possibility of participating in the World Para Equestrian Championships and in the Para Olympics.

The case was initially heard by ODEI – the Equality Tribunal – which found in favour of Para Equestrian Ireland. This finding was appealed to the Circuit Court, which found that victimisation did occur. Victimisation is prohibited under the Equal Status Act. It occurs when a provider of goods and services treats someone adversely because they have made a complaint of discrimination to the Equality Tribunal, because they have been a witness in any proceedings under the Acts or because they have opposed by lawful means an act that is unlawful under the Acts. Joan Salmon had used the media to raise the alleged failure of Para Equestrian Ireland to make reasonable accommodation of her needs. The equality legislation requires a reasonable accommodation of people with disabilities subject to exemption. She was treated adversely because of raising this alleged failure to make reasonable accommodation in the media and was found to have been victimised.

This case is of particular interest in providing insights into relationships that can exist between the individual with disabilities and the voluntary organisations that manage the funds and services they require. Such organisations are covered by the equality legislation. Goodwill, voluntary endeavour and charity cannot replace the need for high standards in meeting obligations under the equality legislation. People with disabilities have rights under the equality legislation in relation to the services provided by such organisations. There can often be expectations of gratitude from people with disabilities held by those providing services where the organisation is based on a charitable model. There is a danger that such expectations can diminish the rights of people with disabilities and their need to exercise these rights assertively and with confidence. These insights from this case hold learning for the wider sector of voluntary organisations providing services to people with disabilities.

Later in 2004 the Equality Authority supported a case on the race ground that was heard by the Labour Court. The case was taken by Aderonke Rasaq, who was dismissed by Campbell Catering on the basis of an allegation that the Labour Court found to be false, that she stole three bananas. The Labour Court found in her favour and awarded her €15,000. Aderonke Rasaq had been employed by Campbell Catering as a catering assistant at a Dublin hostel for refugees. She was in the early stages of pregnancy. Staff were permitted to take as much food as they wished for consumption on the premises. The day before she was dismissed she was feeling nauseous at the end of her shift and took three bananas to eat in the locker room before leaving work. She was dismissed for allegedly stealing company property. She was not told her dismissal was contemplated before the decision was taken. She was not informed of her right to representation at a disciplinary hearing. There was no meaningful investigation of the allegation.

The Labour Court found that she did not steal the bananas and could not reasonably have been accused of doing so. It found the decision to dismiss her was discriminatory on the race ground. The Labour Court also made it clear that non-national workers can encounter particular difficulties in their jobs arising from cultural and linguistic diversity. It identified a positive duty under the legislation on employers to take account of any practical implications of cultural and linguistic diversity in the workforce in the design and development of their disciplinary procedures. The Labour Court clarified that discrimination can occur not only where two people are treated differently despite the circumstances being the same but also where two people are treated the same despite their circumstances being different. Cultural and linguistic difference creates a context where the circumstances of individual workers can be different when it comes to applying disciplinary procedures. If adjustments are not made to take account of this difference discrimination can occur.

This case is of particular interest because of this focus on disciplinary policies and procedures in organisations where the workforce is ethnically diverse. The implications of the Labour Court finding is that all employers should review all their employment policies and procedures to ensure they adequately take account of the cultural and linguistic diversity of staff. This positive duty to accommodate cultural and linguistic diversity now sits alongside the obligation on employers already set out in the equality legislation to make adjustments for and reasonably accommodate employees with disabilities.

In June 2003 the Equality Authority announced that it was initiating proceedings against Portmarnock Golf Club under the Equal Status Act. The Act makes specific provisions in relation to registered clubs – bodies that hold a certificate of registration under the Registration of Clubs Act 1904–99 – which allows clubs to sell alcohol to members and certain visitors. Any person, including the Equality Authority, can apply to the District Court for a declaration that a club is a discriminating club. While there are exemptions, a club will be treated as a discriminating club if it has a rule, policy or practice which discriminates against a member, or applicant or a person involved in its management discriminates against a member or applicant, in relation to the affairs of the club. Portmarnock has a policy of excluding women members.

The Equality Authority applied to the District Court for a declaration that Portmarnock Golf Club is a discriminating golf club. If the District Court found Portmarnock to be a discriminating club it could suspend the club's certificate to sell alcohol for a period of up to 30 days. While a second or subsequent decision that a club is a discriminating club remains in effect no certificate of registration will be granted to or renewed for a club. In February 2004 the District Court found that the club was discriminatory and did not come within the exemption in the Act. The Act exempts clubs where the principal purpose of the club is to cater only for the needs of persons of a particular gender, marital status, family status, sexual orientation, religious belief or none, age, disability, nationality or ethnic or national origin or members of the Traveller community. The District Court found that the principal purpose of the club was to play golf and that a specific need could not be ascribed to men's golf. A decision in relation to suspending the Certificate of Registration was adjourned to await the result of a High Court challenge to the constitutionality of the Act being taken by Portmarnock Golf Club. However, as Portmarnock wished to appeal the finding of the District Court by way of a case stated to the High Court they had to apply to the District Court to decide on this suspension. In May 2004 the District Court suspended Portmarnock Golf Club's licence to sell alcohol for seven days. However, this was not implemented pending the outcome of the High Court proceedings.

In March 2005 the High Court heard Portmarnock Golf Club's appeal of the District Court decision by way of a case stated and Portmarnock Golf Club's challenge to the constitutionality of these provisions of the Equal Status Act. In June 2005 the High Court found in favour of Portmarnock Golf Club in relation to the interpretation of the exemption in the Equal Status Act and declared Portmarnock Golf Club was not a discriminating club. The High Court in effect interpreted men's needs so broadly as to include sporting needs. However, Portmarnock Golf Club were unsuccessful in their Constitutional challenge. It is clear from the judgment that the Constitution does not require the law to protect Portmarnock Golf Club's right to have a male only golf club. The judge also observed that the Constitutional provisions in relation to freedom of association do not preclude the enactment of legislation to achieve equality. These Constitutional elements of the judgment have an importance for any further implementation or development of equality legislation. The Equality Authority has appealed the High Court finding that Portmarnoch Golf Club was not a discriminating club under the Equal Status Act to the Supreme Court.

This case is of interest not just for its focus on registered clubs but also for its relevance to wider ambitions for gender equality in society. It stimulated widespread debate. The exclusion of women members from Portmarnock Golf Club means that women are denied networking opportunities in a club whose membership is made up of powerful businessmen and influential professionals. The capacity of a society to achieve gender equality is diminished in a context where such a significant institution could continue to exclude women. Attitudes that underpin the exclusion of women as reflected in the practice of Portmarnock Golf Club could find expression in a wide range of organisations where many of its members hold senior decision-making positions. This could place further boundaries to achieving gender equality.

These cases illustrate the contribution to change in the situation of people experiencing inequality that can be made by enforcement of the equality legislation. An individual can seek a resolution to their specific experience of discrimination by making a claim under the legislation. The implementation of the legislation makes an important contribution at this level of the individual. The three cases described also highlight how successful enforcement of the legislation can contribute to change at the level of institutions and at societal level.

Cases can have a ripple effect through a sector. The case against Para Equestrian Ireland has relevance for all voluntary sector organisations providing services to people with disabilities. It could stimulate such organisations to review practice in the context of equality legislation and to review the type of relationships that exist between service providers and people with disabilities.

Precedent in relation to interpretation of the equality legislation can be established by cases. The case against Campbell Catering further evolved the understanding of the obligations required of employers by the equality legislation. It could stimulate all organisations to review their employment policies and procedures to ensure they adequately take into account the cultural and linguistic diversity among staff.

Widespread debate across society can be stimulated by cases. The case against Portmarnock Golf Club provides an example of this. It stimulated a debate about gender equality and our commitment as a society to gender equality.

The Equality Authority can contribute to change in support of equality objectives through its work of enforcing the legislation. The Equality Authority does not support all cases that are brought to it. It is involved in strategic litigation which is based on making choices between cases. The Board of the Equality Authority establish criteria from time to time to guide the choices to be made in this regard. These criteria are reviewed on a regular basis.

The criteria established for a strategic litigation approach need to have regard to the potential in each case for individual benefit, for ripple effect across sectors or geographical areas, for precedent setting that will expand the understanding and interpretation of the legislation and for stimulating the wide debate on equality that will shape the cultural change that is necessary if a more equal society is to emerge. Not all cases will be high profile or precedent setting. The criteria established for strategic litigation should include a focus on building a culture of compliance. Employers and service providers need to be clear that where discrimination happens enforcement will follow. The legislation needs to be seen to be regularly enforced or it will fail to have any significant impact. Enforcement work by the Equality Authority therefore needs to involve a critical mass of casework to be brought forward on an ongoing basis across a range of sectors and issues.

In the first five years of its operation the Equality Authority prioritised casework through strategic litigation in its enforcement role. This was important given how new and groundbreaking the equality legislation was, and given the need to develop a body of casework under the legislation. It was also important given the high level of expectation from people within groups across the nine grounds experiencing inequality that the new legislation would address their individual experiences of discrimination. However, with time, it will be important to incorporate strategic litigation in a wider approach of strategic enforcement which makes use of the full range of powers available to the Equality Authority.

The Equality Authority in a strategic enforcement approach would be involved in the provision of legal representation to claimants, the taking of cases in its own name, the preparation of codes of practice, conducting equality reviews and preparing action plans, and conducting inquiries. In the strategic enforcement approach it is necessary to find the most effective mix across these different powers to support enforcement for change in a manner that contributes to the achievement of equality objectives. There are, however, resource constraints to developing a strategic enforcement approach. In particular equality reviews and inquiries are costly exercises. The development of an effective strategic enforcement approach will in part depend on the adequacy of resources available to the Equality Authority.

EQUALITY AUTHORITY – NEGOTIATION FOR CHANGE

Three initiatives illustrate what negotiation for change is about and the potential impact this strand of activity can hold. The initiatives described reflect the breadth of the work of the Equality Authority. They cover multi-ground approaches and single ground approaches to equality. They encompass the public and the private sectors. They address the workplace and the provision of goods and services. The three initiatives focus on equality in education, workplace equality and reasonable accommodation of people with disabilities.

In 2003 the Minister for Education and Science launched Schools and the Equal Status Act. This was a joint publication of the Equality Authority and the Department of Education and Science. The core objective of the publication was to inform schools of their obligations under the Equal Status Act and to highlight steps that could be taken to gear up to meet these obligations. The Department of Education and Science distributed the booklet to all schools at primary and post-primary levels.

The publication sets out the provisions of the Equal Status Act as they applied to schools. It identifies the importance of creating an inclusive school and sets out an understanding of what is meant by an inclusive school. It states:

> The inclusive school prevents and combats discrimination. It is one that respects, values and accommodates diversity across all nine grounds in the equality legislation – gender, marital status, family status, sexual orientation, religion, age, disability, race and membership of the Traveller community. It seeks positive experiences, a sense of belonging and outcomes for all students across the nine grounds. Outcomes include access, participation, personal development and achieving education credentials.[20]

Opportunities for action in moving towards the inclusive school are identified in the publication. The school development plan can include equality objectives and the steps to be taken to achieve these and can identify the particular educational needs of students from across the nine grounds. The admissions policy can ensure no student is denied a place in the school because of their membership of a group under any of the nine grounds and can identify the measures the school will take to achieve maximum accessibility and ensure the principles of equality. The school code of behaviour can require behaviour that respects diversity across the nine grounds. It can prohibit sexual harassment and harassment and set out procedures to deal with such incidents if they occur. It can identify actions to prevent such incidents.

Subsequent to this joint publication the Equality Authority has worked with the schools' inspectorate to develop and pilot an approach to including an explicit equality focus in whole school evaluation. It has agreed to work with the National Educational Welfare Board to support a focus on sexual harassment and harassment in guidance to be developed on school codes of behaviour. It is working to develop a joint initiative with the School Planning Development Initiative for second level schools to support the inclusion of an equality focus in school development plans.

The Programme for Prosperity and Fairness national agreement was negotiated by the social partners and the government for the period 2000 to 2002. In this the social partners committed 'to the development of equal opportunities policies and practices and will encourage and support their development in every practical way'.[21] A framework committee was established 'in response to the challenges faced by both employers and unions arising from the implementation of the Employment Equality Act 1998 and in assisting the promotion of equal opportunities in the workplace'.[22] This has been convened and supported by the Equality Authority and includes IBEC, Congress, the Department of Finance, the Department of Justice, Equality and Law Reform, the Local Government Management Services Board, the Health Service Executive – Employers agency (formerly the Health Service Employers Agency) and the Equality Diversity Network.

Over these three years (2000–02) the Framework Committee supported initiatives to develop practical approaches to a range of equality themes within clusters or networks of enterprises and organisations. Themes worked on included the recruitment and retention of older workers, the management of diversity, the promotion of good practice in relation to equality and the promotion of human resource policies and practices that are positive to the creation of opportunities for people with disabilities. The committee published guidance for enterprises on putting in place employment equality policies and on providing equality and diversity training. Congress developed an accredited equality and diversity course in partnership with Dublin City University Business School that targeted trade union activists with the support of the committee. IBEC developed a resource for diversity management and disseminated this among their members with the support of the committee. The Civil Service Equality Unit in the Department of Finance were supported to disseminate and encourage implementation of a new Gender Equality Policy.

The Framework Committee was re-established under the Sustaining Progress national agreement (2003–05). This agreement stated: 'The work of the committee will include: developing and disseminating practical supports for the equal opportunities workplace, supporting individual projects and engaging with equality planning and equality reviews.'[23]

The core focus agreed by the re-established Framework Committee was to support planned and systematic approaches to workplace equality. The Framework Committee supported institutional development external to the enterprise with a capacity to stimulate and support enterprise level initiatives to promote equality. The committee provided funding to business networks and trade unions to develop their contribution to workplace equality. It supported institutional development internal to enterprises in order to develop a planned and systematic approach to workplace equality. The committee funded small and medium enterprises to put in place employment equality policies and equality and diversity training for staff as a means of developing a planned and systematic approach to workplace equality.

In October 2003 the National Centre for Partnership and Performance, at the request of the Government, established the Forum on the Workplace of the Future. The aim of the Forum was to foster in-depth debate on how the world of work can best adapt to competitive pressures, improve the delivery of services and respond to the changing needs and preferences of all employees. In its work with the Forum the Equality Authority made the case that 'our ability to mobilize, retain and develop diverse sources of labour supply will be a crucial determinant of the future growth rate of the economy' and that 'workplace policies and practices to promote equality of opportunity, to accommodate diversity and to combat discrimination have played, and will continue to play, an essential part in mobilising and developing this diverse labour supply'.[24] The Equality Authority brought many of the ideas developed and tested through the framework committee to the deliberations of the Forum. These included ideas in relation to planned and systematic approaches to equality, developing a workplace equality infrastructure including equality policies and equality and diversity training, and the need for a support infrastructure to be available to enterprises to assist in developing effective approaches to combating discrimination and promoting equality. These ideas were being brought to a Forum whose membership overlapped with that of the Framework Committee.

The Equal Status Act requires providers of goods and services, accommodation, educational establishments and registered clubs to accommodate the needs of people with disabilities through making reasonable changes in what they do and how they do it, where without these changes it would be very difficult or impossible for people with disabilities to obtain those goods or services. This requirement does not apply if it costs more than a nominal amount. This important provision is unique in the legislation in imposing a positive duty on service providers. It formed the basis for a single ground initiative which included joint work between the Equality Authority and the Library Council.

This joint work started with the publication of guidance for libraries on approaches to making reasonable accommodation for customers with disabilities. This began from the premise that such approaches 'need to be integrated into all areas of service provision. This means that all existing services – from reference collections to children's storytelling, from local history to membership forms – should be examined in order to determine whether they contribute to inclusivity or inhibit it.'[25]

The guidance identifies a range of areas for action on making reasonable accommodation for customers with disabilities. Consultation with people with disabilities and disability organisations is a key starting point The organisation's commitment to customers with disabilities and the steps to be taken to ensure their inclusion should be set out in a disability policy. Disability audits should be carried out to identify the presence of people with disabilities in the local community, to assess current services for accessibility and relevance to people with disabilities and their needs, and to identify relevant staff skills, knowledge and experience in communicating effectively and making reasonable accommodation for people with disabilities. Inclusive design of the physical environment and of the organisation and delivery of services is important in making reasonable accommodation for customers with disabilities. Training should be provided to develop staff skills and support staff attitudes to assist in engaging effectively with people with disabilities. Marketing strategies that identify people with disabilities as a specific customer base and quality control that assesses the presence and participation of customers with disabilities should also be developed.

The guidelines provided the basis for joint initiatives with four county libraries to pilot their implementation. These initiatives started with training designed to explore and build on the knowledge of key personnel about disability issues and to design strategies for local action. Kildare Library and Arts Service provided staff training, developed a staff manual and built contact with local disability groups, and branch libraries developed work programmes on reasonable accommodation of people with disabilities. A process of consultation with people with disabilities on plans for the new central library was organised by Cavan Library Service. Dublin City Public Libraries developed a disability handbook for staff, disability proofed library building maintenance programmes and reviewed library purchasing policy from a disability perspective. Mayo Library Service established liaison with disability organisations, made small scale improvements to libraries and allocated a budget to improve the relevance of library collections for people with disabilities.

These pilot projects have created the potential for a duplication of this initiative with a range of other county libraries. They have opened up a debate within libraries on making a wider accommodation of diversity – making adjustments to cater for the practical implications of difference across the nine grounds covered by the equality legislation. The pilot projects have also provided a gateway to developing similar work within the local authorities where the library services are located. The Equality Authority has developed joint work on the reasonable accommodation of people with disabilities with Kildare County Council and Cavan County Council.

Two shared elements can be identified in these three initiatives that shape this approach of negotiation for change. These are the elements of partnership and leadership. Partnership is the first key element. The key actors in relation to an issue or area of work were identified by the Equality Authority which then negotiated an entry point with each partner. Negotiating an entry point is not about seeking favours or a generosity of response to the challenge of equality from the organisation with whom partnership is sought. Rather it is about identifying how partnership might assist this organisation in solving problems they face or meeting commitments they have made. The Department of Education and Science work within a legislative context that requires a significant focus on equality within school provision. Congress and IBEC had made commitments in the Programme for Prosperity and Fairness to supporting equal opportunities workplaces. The Library Council was committed to libraries serving as a space for all. All organisations were subject to new and challenging obligations under equality legislation.

A further important phase of partnership is the negotiation of a shared understanding to guide and shape joint work. The concept of the inclusive school provided the core shared understanding of the joint work between the Equality Authority and the Department of Education and Science. The concept of planned and systematic approaches to workplace equality emerged after the first three years as the shared understanding with the social partners in the Equal Opportunities Framework Committee. Reasonable accommodation of customers with disabilities was both the starting point and the shared understanding for the Equality Authority and the Library Council in their joint work.

Leadership is the second key element in this approach. Each partner made an important constituency available for the joint work being developed with the Equality Authority. The Department of Education and Science provided an access to primary and post primary schools. Access to private and public sector employers and trade unions was provided by the social partners. The Library Council provided access to the libraries. The leadership provided by these organisations opened up a respected and accepted channel of communication about equality issues within these constituencies.

The leadership provided by the partners in these joint ventures created the potential for guiding change. Each of the initiatives involved the development of guidance materials for their constituencies. The dissemination of guidance materials with the imprimatur and the involvement of a diversity of partners has a capacity to be more acceptable and more relevant to each different constituency because of the leadership played by these partners organisation within their constituencies. The guidance material developed included publications on school initiatives to support compliance with Equal Status legislation, guidance on employment equality policies and on equality and diversity training for enterprises and guidance on approaches to making reasonable accommodation for library users with disabilities.

A final dimension to leadership involves the partnership opening up possibilities for new work by the Equality

Authority. The Library Council and the county libraries provided a gateway into the local authorities where a new set of partnerships were developed. A gateway into the school's inspectorate and the School Development Planning Initiative where further partnerships were established was provided by the Department of Education and Science.

There are potential pitfalls in this approach of negotiation for change. The work takes time to progress. The building of partnership takes time and care. Different organisations with different core mandates working together can move at a slower pace than that which could be achieved by a single organisation. The work can be cautious. The scope of shared commitment established by the partner organisations can be pitched too narrowly. The shared understanding can reflect a lowest common denominator rather than new ambition to be shared.

The potential benefit of negotiation for change rests on the creation of shared responsibility for promoting equality and combating discrimination. This is key to making progress – significant institutions across society take on to advance equality objectives as part of pursuing their own core business. The Equality Authority uses its limited resources as a catalyst, to develop this shared responsibility with partner organisations for the achievement of equality objectives – a shared responsibility that can result in a much greater impact than could be made by a single organisation working on its own.

EQUALITY AUTHORITY - CULTURAL ACTION FOR CHANGE

Public education and public information initiatives can contribute to cultural change. Cultural change work involves the Equality Authority in challenging negative stereotypes of groups experiencing inequality, in celebrating diversity in society and the benefits of this diversity for society, and in stimulating a broad commitment to equality objectives. The Anti-Racist Workplace Week initiative is described as an example of this work.

In November 2001 billboards around the country proclaimed:

no application
no interview
the job's yours...
work against racism

November 2002, and billboards around the country carried pictures of an emigrant Irish staff nurse in Bahrain and a migrant worker staff nurse from the Philippines in Carlow Regional Hospital along with the message:

It works both ways
For migrant workers
Work against racism

The challenge to work against racism reappeared on billboards around the country in November 2004 suggesting:

Together Ireland is working
Don't let racism obstruct us

Each time the message was backed up by infomercials on the issue of combating racism on local and national radio.

These three public education campaigns marked a significant engagement by the Equality Authority in public awareness work. The campaigns reflected a growing concern at new levels of and a new virulence to racism being experienced by Black and minority ethnic people, including Travellers. They focused on the workplace. The workplace was identified as a microcosm of the wider society. Racism can be imported from this wider society and find expression in the workplace. Racism can also be effectively challenged within the workplace and the impact of this can reach out into the wider society. The campaigns were designed to stimulate a public debate about the new multi-cultural Ireland and how increased cultural diversity in Ireland is a source of creativity and needs to be valued.

Public education campaigns can contribute to cultural change. They support a popular consciousness that deems racism to be unacceptable and that celebrates cultural diversity. However, even carefully crafted messages gain limited foothold over the longer term unless they are linked to more practical action-based endeavour. The partnership that implemented these campaigns provided the opportunity to link public education and practical action. By 2004 this partnership included Congress, IBEC, the Construction Industry Federation, the Small Firms Association, the Chambers of Commerce of Ireland, the Irish Farmers Association and the Department of Justice, Equality and Law Reform along with the Equality Authority. The public education campaigns form part of an annual Anti-Racist Workplace Week organised by the partners. The week is a focal point for the partner organisations and their members to take practical steps to celebrate cultural diversity and to put in train longer term actions and strategies to ensure their workplaces:

- are free from discrimination;
- are welcoming to Black and minority ethnic people (including Travellers);
- make adjustments for and value cultural diversity;
- take steps to achieve full equality in practice for Black and minority ethnic employees;
- send out a message for greater equality across local communities and the wider society.

Anti-Racist Workplace Week provided opportunities for leadership on the issues of racism. IBEC encouraged employers to take a lead in combating racism in the workplace. Congress raised concerns about the design of the work permit system for migrant workers. The IFA highlighted the importance of migrant workers to the rural economy and pointed out that the farm environment faced the same challenges in relation to cultural diversity as any other workplace. The Equality Authority highlighted the disturbing growth in cases of alleged discrimination under the Employment Equality Acts on the race ground and the range of very difficult situations being experienced by migrant workers.

Cultural action for change has involved the Equality Authority in a range of public education campaigns. These campaigns have also focused on ageism, on work life balance and on the equality legislation itself. Cultural action for change has also involved the Equality Authority in a wider range of initiatives. A public information centre provides information to the public on the equality legislation and on maternity protection, adoptive leave and parental leave legislation. Media liaison has sought a public profile for the Equality Authority and its work. Media coverage of cases supported by the Equality Authority has made a particular contribution to their ripple effect beyond the individual complainant or respondent. The publicity around individual cases supports a wider understanding of obligations under the equality legislation and stimulates change beyond the particular claimant or respondent involved in the specific case.

EQUALITY AUTHORITY – KNOWLEDGE DEVELOPMENT FOR CHANGE

Research work and dialogue with groups experiencing inequality both contribute to knowledge development for the change necessary for the achievement of equality objectives. The work of knowledge development involves initiatives to produce new information about and analysis of equality issues and strategies, and about experiences and situations of inequality. Two such initiatives are described. The first is a research project commissioned by the Equality Authority on transsexual people and the second is a report entitled *Implementing Equality for Gay, Lesbian and Bisexual People*, published by the Equality Authority with the assistance of an advisory committee which included the participation of gay and lesbian organisations.

In 2004 the Equality Authority published a research report, *Access to Health Services for Transsexual People*. The report was groundbreaking as no evidence was found of any previous research on the circumstances of transsexual people in Ireland or on 'transsexualism' as an issue in Ireland. It concluded that 'transsexual health care is not well provided for in Irish health policy at present and that transsexual people encounter significant difficulties in accessing appropriate health care'.[26]

Information on the legal situation of transsexual people was provided with the report pointing out that there is no provision for transsexual people to be officially recognised in the gender in which they identify.[27] As a consequence transsexual people do not have a right to marry in their adopted gender or to change their birth certificate or to enjoy any right legally confined to the gender to which they feel they belong. Some protection against discrimination is afforded to transsexual people under the equality legislation.

The report provided challenging insights into healthcare policy and practice in relation to transsexuals. Most health boards contacted confined their provision to funding genital reassignment surgery abroad through the treatment abroad scheme rather than provision of the more complete treatment path required by transsexuals involving general practitioners, psychiatric services, hormonal therapy, surgical interventions and non-medical services such as speech therapy and electrolysis. Transsexual people do have access to General Practitioners and psychiatric services. The need for professional training on transsexual issues for psychiatrists and General Practitioners was highlighted in the research as was the need to develop quality standards and procedures for treatment.

A unique insight into the perspectives of transsexuals was afforded by the report. All but one of those surveyed had begun questioning their gender identity before the age of 15. They reported the lack of knowledge among professionals about the condition and about where to refer people. They highlighted barriers to accessing support and treatment including geographic accessibility, lack of information and lack of family services. The negative impact of the lack of service provision was defined in terms of depression, suicidal feelings and, in some cases people accessing hormones on the 'black market' which were expensive and potentially dangerous without medical supervision.

The report was launched at a time of significant policy development, legislative change and institutional restructuring within the Health Service. While this may make it difficult to focus in on a new policy it does create a context of opportunity for change. The report should lead to a naming of transsexual people in health policy along with a dialogue between health providers/policy makers and transsexual people and their organisations.

Equality focused research contributes to knowledge development for change in a range of ways. It can explore current institutional practice and identify improvements that would enhance equality outcomes. Research of this nature done by the Equality Authority has included research on family friendly working arrangements in the small and medium enterprise sector, on the gathering and analysis of equality data across the nine grounds and on recruitment practices for people with disabilities in the public service.

Research can identify and document good equality practice within organisations thus securing a wider dissemination of information about such practice. The Equality Authority's published research on good practice includes research on managing cultural diversity in the workplace and on making adjustments for older people, Travellers and other minority ethnic people and people with disabilities in the provision of labour market training and education programmes.

Policy issues can be illuminated by research. Research initiatives can support new analysis, understanding and perspectives on policy issues that can shape and influence policy thinking, policy making and policy implementation. Partnership rights of same sex couples, the interface between poverty and equality and transsexual people's access to health services have been subjects for Equality Authority research projects seeking to make such a contribution.

Finally, research can generate evidence against which progress on equality issues can be assessed and from which new policy priorities can be identified. This research is often quantitative but can also be qualitative in a context where limited data is available across many of the nine grounds. The Equality Authority carried out research of this kind on the participation of Travellers, people with disabilities and older people in the labour market.

In 2002 the Equality Authority published a report, *Implementing Equality for Lesbians, Gays and Bisexuals.*[28] This report was a comprehensive exploration of the situation and experience of gay, bisexual and lesbian people. It made recommendations for change across eight different policy areas – community development and empowerment, equality proofing, partnership rights, health, education, youth services, employment and training services and violence and harassment. Three key themes are identified as emerging from the recommendations:

- the need to mainstream lesbian, gay and bisexual (LGB) people's situation, experience and identity into the design, delivery and implementation of social policy and services;
- the need to resource the participation of LGB people so that they can engage with policy makers and service deliverers and where necessary to target the LGB community with regard to capacity building initiatives;
- the recognition of same sex partnerships with regard to parenting, inheritance, property, healthcare, pensions and immigration.

The report was prepared for the Equality Authority by an advisory committee established under the equality legislation. The legislation provides for the Equality Authority to appoint advisory committees to advise it on matters relating to its functions for such a period and with such terms of reference it thinks appropriate. In this instance the Equality Authority appointed a time-limited advisory committee made up of representatives of lesbian, gay and bisexual non-governmental organisations, academics, social partners and government departments. Its terms of reference were:

a) to identify examples of best practice, drawing from experience in other jurisdictions, in promoting equality under the sexual orientation ground;
b) to develop a perspective to inform policy making on equality in employment and service provision for gay, lesbian and bisexual people; and actions to give effect to this perspective; and to propose a programme of action;
c) to recommend what role the Equality Authority should undertake in relation to the sexual orientation ground.[29]

The report stimulated a new visibility to the identity, experience and situation of lesbian, gay and bisexual people. It set out the change needed if equality was to be progressed under the sexual orientation ground. It contributed to a new consensus in support of this change. The National Economic and Social Forum considered the report and produced its own report to support implementation of the recommendations made. This report emphasised the issue of partnership rights. The case established for partnership rights rested predominantly on the disadvantages that accrue to gay and lesbian couples in the absence of legal recognition of same sex partnerships. These include disadvantages in relation to pensions, tax, parenting, succession and immigration. The case is also made on the basis that Ireland now lags behind its EU counterparts in achieving 'parity for same sex couples'.[30] This focus on parity also suggests another core rationale for partnership rights based on the need for an equality of recognition. Equality for lesbian and gay people will remain a distant aspiration as long as their relationships are not valued and accorded a status on a par with heterosexual relationships.

Implementing Equality for Lesbians, Gays and Bisexuals served as a powerful stimulus to debate on this issue of partnership rights. The National Economic and Social Forum's subsequent report raised partnership rights for same sex couples as a core issue. The Law Reform Commission has addressed the issue in its work on cohabiting couples. Political parties have taken stands in favour of partnership rights with Fine Gael producing a policy document on the issue. A Private Members Bill on the issue is being brought forward in the Seanad by Senator David Norris.

The work of the advisory committee highlights the contribution of participation by groups experiencing inequality to knowledge development for change. The advisory committee process is essentially about participation and bringing forward the knowledge held by those who experience inequality and discrimination. The range of organisations involved in the advisory committee allowed this knowledge to be shaped, developed and organised in support of necessary change. A similar initiative was developed by the Equality Authority on implementing equality for older people and is currently being deployed in relation to carers.

FUTURE PERSPECTIVES

The Equality Authority is a core institution within the strategic framework for action on equality in that it is charged under equality legislation with the promotion of equality and combating of discrimination. This is the institution with a significant responsibility for stimulating a focus on equality, for driving forward the change needed for society and its institutions to be characterised by equality, and for supporting other organisations to put into practice an ambition for equality. This chapter has set out how the Equality Authority has sought to play its role in this regard – both in terms of strategy deployed and in terms of the analysis developed of some of the core equality issues.

Four key strands of activity for change are identified in the work of the Equality Authority in promoting equality of opportunity and combating discrimination. These strands do not stand alone as separate areas of endeavour but are inter-linked. The strands are:

- enforcement for change;
- negotiation for change;
- cultural action for change;
- knowledge development for change.

The Equality Authority has defined this necessary change in terms of creating a society that offers a new access to resources, to participation in decision making, to an acknowledgement, a valuing and an accommodation of their different identities, experiences and situations and to relationships of care, love and solidarity for those groups currently experiencing inequality. The Equality Authority has further defined this necessary change in terms of institutions that are free from discrimination, make adjustments for difference and take positive action for equality.

Persistent and significant inequalities suggest the need for further development of the current strategic framework for action on equality and of its constituent dimensions. The Equality Authority forms part of the institutional dimension to this strategic framework. The enforcement powers, functions and structure of the Equality Authority could usefully be further developed.

The Equality Authority has already highlighted where its enforcement powers could be further developed in submissions to the Minister for Justice, Equality and Law Reform. These recommendations include the need to be able to seek inter-locutory relief from the High Court or Circuit Court in urgent cases where the powers afforded to the ODEI – The Equality Tribunal – are insufficient to grant a necessary, immediate and effective remedy. This power would be valuable in addressing situations of discrimination in such as job interviews or in admission to a school. Discrimination in such instances has serious implications for the life chances of the person involved. There is a need for an immediate remedy in these examples if long term disadvantage is not to result from delays in securing redress.

In relation to its functions the Equality Authority has recommended that it should have the function of keeping legislative proposals and policy changes under review. This would allow the Equality Authority to identify any implications of new legislation or policy for the promotion of equality of opportunity and the elimination of discrimination in the areas covered by equality legislation. It would provide early access for the Equality Authority to proposed legislative and policy changes and would enable the Equality Authority to contribute to a coherence for all legislation and policy making with established equality objectives. Such a function would have been particularly important in the development of legislation and policy initiatives such as the recent National Disability Strategy.

In relation to structure, the Equality Authority must grapple with the challenge of meeting the demand from local community groups and individuals for the Equality Authority to have a local presence. The issue of a local presence is important for any national institution based in a single location. A local presence is required to facilitate a two way communication with local communities. This is necessary so that there is a local awareness of the work, functions and powers of the Equality Authority and so that the Equality Authority has access to the concerns, perspectives and knowledge of local communities. It is also necessary to stimulate and support a local advocacy for equality that would enhance the effective implementation of equality legislation.

The model the Equality Authority has pursued is effectively about a 'virtual' local presence. It depends in particular on a partnership with the Citizens Information Centres. The centres provide and distribute Equality Authority materials. With the support of Comhairle, the staff and volunteers in the centres have been trained in equality issues and the equality legislation. Two centres have hosted regular legal clinics with Equality Authority staff and two centres have provided direct support to claimants seeking redress under the equality legislation. A number of other State agencies have developed similar relationships with the Citizens Information Centres. This is a model with significant potential to meet the challenge for a local presence. It would, however, require further investment and development in the Citizen Information Centres and agreement on an expanded role for them.

NOTES

1. *Annual Report 2003*, Equality Authority (Dublin) 2004
2. *Annual Report 2002*, Equality Authority (Dublin) 2003
3. *Annual Report 2001*, Equality Authority (Dublin) 2002
4. *Annual Report 2000*, Equality Authority (Dublin) 2001
5. Zappone, K. *Charting the Equality Agenda*, Equality Authority and Equality Commission for Northern Ireland (Dublin) 2001
6. *Women and Men in Ireland 2004.* Central Statistics Office (Dublin) 2004
7. Zappone, K. (ed.) *Rethinking Identity*, Joint Equality and Human Rights Forum (Dublin) 2003
8. Pierce, M. *Minority Ethnic People with Disabilities in Ireland*, Equality Authority (Dublin) 2003
9. *Strategic Plan 2003–2005*, Equality Authority (Dublin) 2003
10. *Code of Practice on Sexual Harassment and Harassment at Work*, Equality Authority (Dublin) 2002
11. Barry, E. 'Different Hierarchies – Enforcing Equality Law', in *Equality in Diversity – The New Equality Directives*, Edited by Cathryn Costelloe and Eilis Barry, Irish Centre for European Law/Equality Authority (Dublin) 2003
12. Barry, E. 'Different Hierarchies – Enforcing Equality Law', in *Equality in Diversity – The New Equality Directives*, Edited by Cathryn Costelloe and Eilis Barry, Irish Centre for European Law/Equality Authority (Dublin) 2003
13. *Equality in a Diverse Ireland, Strategic Plan 2000–2002*, Equality Authority (Dublin) 2000
14. *Equality in a Diverse Ireland, Strategic Plan 2000–2002*, Equality Authority (Dublin) 2000
15. *Equality in a Diverse Ireland, Strategic Plan 2000–2002*, Equality Authority (Dublin) 2000
16. *Equality in a Diverse Ireland, Strategic Plan 2000–2002*, Equality Authority (Dublin) 2000
17. *Equality in a Diverse Ireland, Strategic Plan 2000–2002*, Equality Authority (Dublin) 2000
18. *Strategic Plan 2003–2005*, Equality Authority (Dublin) 2003
19. *Strategic Plan 2003–2005*, Equality Authority (Dublin) 2003
20. *Schools and the Equal Status Act*, Equality Authority and Department of Education and Science (Dublin) 2003
21. *Programme for Prosperity and Fairness*, The Stationery Office (Dublin) 1999
22. *Programme for Prosperity and Fairness*, The Stationery Office (Dublin) 1999
23. *Sustaining Progress – Social Partnership Agreement 2003–2005*, The Stationery Office (Dublin) 2002
24. *Building an Inclusive Workplace*, Equality Authority (Dublin) 2004
25. Library Access. Equality Authority and Library Council (Dublin) 2003.
26. Collins, E. and Sheehan, B. *Access to Health Sources for Transsexual*

People, Equality Authority (Dublin) 2004

27. *Implementing Equality for Lesbians Gays and Bisexuals*, Equality Authority (Dublin) 2004

28. *Implementing Equality for Lesbians Gays and Bisexuals*, Equality Authority (Dublin) 2004

29. *Implementing Equality for Lesbians Gays and Bisexuals*, Equality Authority (Dublin) 2004

30. *Implementing Equality for Lesbians Gays and Bisexuals*, Equality Authority (Dublin) 2004

Chapter Three

Legislating for Equality

EQUALITY LEGISLATION AND THE STRATEGIC FRAMEWORK

Equality legislation is another important dimension of the strategic framework for action on equality. It can set out a key foundation of rights from which change in experiences and situations of inequality can be progressed. By doing so it can set the parameters for the ambition for equality to be achieved through the strategic framework. It can provide a statutory basis to all other dimensions to the framework including institutions, targeting, mainstreaming, participation and monitoring. By doing so it can secure a continuity of implementation to these dimensions and an ongoing impact from their implementation.

Equality legislation can prohibit discrimination with minimal exemptions. It can require a proactive approach to the promotion of equality. Enforceable rights for particular groups experiencing inequality can be established in equality legislation. Such legislation can seek to achieve change in the economic and social circumstances of those experiencing inequality and exclusion and can provide a valuable affirmation of the importance of diversity for society.

Irish equality legislation includes the Employment Equality Acts 1998 and 2004 and the Equal Status Acts 2000 to 2004. The Employment Equality Acts prohibit discrimination in the workplace on grounds of gender, marital status, family status, age, disability, sexual orientation, race, religion and member-ship of the Traveller community. The Equal Status Acts prohibit discrimination in the provision of goods and services, accommodation and educational establishments on the same nine grounds. The Equal Status Acts contain specific provisions in relation to registered clubs.

A core feature of this equality legislation is that, except for some provisions, it is predominantly comparator based. Discrimination is defined in terms of less favourable treatment on any of the grounds than another person is, has been or would be treated in a comparable situation. For example, this would include a situation where a Traveller child was refused admission to a school where a settled child in a comparable situation was admitted. The legislation does allow for a hypothetical comparator. However it does not address situations of adverse treatment which are connected to any of the grounds where there is no actual or hypothetical comparator. For example, the legislation does not address situations of poor treatment of mental health patients in institutional settings where no comparator from within the ground is available.

While the equality legislation contains remedies that go beyond individual enforcement, it is predominantly based on an individual enforcement model. It allows individuals to bring civil actions to challenge individual experiences of discrimination. This legislation does contain provisions requiring a reasonable accommodation (with exemptions) of people with disabilities. However, beyond this it does not encompass any requirements on employers or service providers to be proactive in promoting equality. Positive action is, however, allowed.

Another related feature of this equality legislation is that it is predominantly based on retrospective fault finding. An incident occurs, an allegation of discrimination is made which is then investigated prior to a finding being made. This is essentially an adversarial approach. Again the legislation, outside of provisions in relation to the vicarious liability of employers and service providers, does not require a proactive approach to equality that would also ensure the incident did not happen in the first place.

The Equality Authority was established under the equality legislation with a statutory mandate to work towards the elimination of discrimination and promotion of equality of opportunity in matters covered by the legislation. The work of the Equality Authority was introduced in the previous chapter.

The equality legislation also established the Equality Tribunal (formerly ODEI) with duties to mediate cases or to investigate cases, hearing all persons interested and desiring to be heard and issuing a decision and providing for redress.

In this chapter the scope and provisions of the Employment Equality Acts and the Equal Status Acts will be set out. Trends in the casefiles of the Equality Authority will be explored. The work of the Equality Tribunal will be introduced. Initiatives that sought to expand the provisions of the legislation and the pressures that the legislation has been subject to will be analysed. Finally some future perspectives on the further development of the legislation will be traced out.

EQUALITY LEGISLATION – SCOPE AND PROVISIONS

Scope

The Employment Equality Acts cover all aspects of the employment relationship from advertising the job to dismissal from the job. Recruitment, equal pay, working conditions, promotion, work experience and vocational training are all covered by the Acts.

The Acts apply to full time, part time and temporary employees, to public and private sector employment, to vocational training bodies, to employment agencies, to trade unions and professional bodies, and to self-employed, partnerships and people employed in another person's home.

The Equal Status Acts apply to the provision of goods and services. Specific provisions are made in relation to educational establishments and in relation to access to and disposal of accommodation. The Acts cover the public and the private sectors. There are separate provisions on registered clubs. Claims of discrimination in relation to licensed premises are now dealt with in the District Court under the Intoxicating Liquor Act 2003.

Provisions of Both Acts

Both Acts make provisions in relation to a range of common

issues. The core elements address discrimination, sexual harassment and harassment, reasonable accommodation of people with disabilities, victimisation and positive action. Both Acts contain a range of exemptions. These different elements are now explored.

Discrimination

Both the Employment Equality Acts 1998 and 2004 and the Equal Status Acts 2000 to 2004 prohibit discrimination including indirect discrimination and discrimination by association. Discrimination is defined as the treatment of a person in a less favourable way than another person is, has been or would be treated in a comparable situation on any of the nine grounds, the membership of which exists, existed, may exist in the future or is imputed to the person concerned.

Indirect discrimination occurs where there is less favourable treatment in effect or by impact. It happens where, for example, people are refused access to employment or a service, not explicitly on account of a discriminatory reason, but because of a provision, practice or requirement which they find hard to satisfy. If the provision, practice or requirement puts people who belong to one of the grounds covered by the Acts at a particular disadvantage then the employer or service provider will have indirectly discriminated unless the provision is objectively justified by a legitimate aim and the means of achieving that aim are appropriate and necessary. This latter element in effect allows some forms of discrimination.

During 2004 the Equality Tribunal made a finding of indirect discrimination against Bus Éireann. This finding illustrates the meaning of indirect discrimination. It was significant given that there are very few recommendations of the Equality Tribunal or the Labour Court on indirect discrimination. Indirect discrimination has an important capacity, within limits, to focus on institutional systems and practices that can be discriminatory.

Brian O'Loughlin took the case against Bus Éireann with the support of the Equality Authority. He had worked as a bus driver for twenty-three years. He availed of a voluntary severance package with effect from 31st October 2001. On

16th October 2001, before leaving the company he asked to be considered for a position of school bus driver and/or seasonal bus driver. He subsequently applied for such work but received a response stating that it was not company policy to re-employ staff who go out on retirement.

The company policy applied to all prospective employees. However 96.5% of those who applied for the voluntary severance package were over 50 years old. The Equality Tribunal found that Bus Éireann did not show how cost savings can be achieved by not employing the complainant who availed of the voluntary severance scheme as opposed to employing someone who had not availed of the scheme. The Equality Tribunal also found that Bus Éireann could not rely on the justification of achieving cost savings (if there were any) for the operation of a policy of not employing persons who availed of voluntary severance. Bus Éireann have appealed this decision.

Discrimination by association happens where a person associated with another person (belonging to a specified ground) is treated less favourably because of that association.

Sexual Harassment and Harassment

Both the Employment Equality Acts and the Equal Status Acts prohibit sexual harassment and harassment. Employees are protected from sexual harassment and harassment by the employer or by anyone the employer might reasonably expect them to come in contact with in the course of their job. Customers, clients, pupils and service users are protected from sexual harassment and harassment when they seek to use goods or services, obtain accommodation or attend educational establishments. Sexual harassment and harassment are important concepts to be defined and prohibited in the legislation. It can be difficult for people who have experienced sexual harassment or harassment to raise the issue. Their experience can be trivialised or ignored. Yet sexual harassment and harassment can have a devastating effect on those who experience it.

Harassment is any form of unwanted conduct related to any of the nine grounds. Sexual harassment is any form of unwanted verbal, non-verbal or physical conduct of a sexual nature. In both cases it is conduct which has the purpose or effect of violating a person's dignity and creating an intimidating, hostile, degrading, humiliating or offensive environment for the person. This conduct can include such as comments, gestures behaviours or the display or circulation of written material or pictures.

It is a defence for an employer to prove that they took reasonable practicable steps to prevent the person harassing or sexually harassing the victim or, where relevant, to prevent the victim from being treated differently by reason of rejecting or accepting the harassment. The Equality Authority has published a Code of Practice on sexual harassment and harassment in the workplace which provides guidance on the steps that need to be taken in this regard.

A person who is responsible for the operation of an educational establishment or where goods, facilities or services are offered to the public or a person who provides accommodation must ensure that any person who has a right to be there is not sexually harassed or harassed. Again the responsible person will be liable for the sexual harassment or harassment unless he or she took reasonably practicable steps to prevent it.

The Equality Tribunal made an important finding of sexual harassment in a case in 2004. A woman was employed as a cleaner in a shopping centre. A security guard employed by another company in the shopping centre began making crude and sexually offensive remarks to her and her female colleagues. One evening he pushed the complainant into the canteen, pulled down her trousers and underwear and struck her a number of times on the bottom.

The incident was witnessed by the complainant's company supervisor who dismissed it as only messing and only a joke. The woman reported the matter to the Gardaí but dropped this complaint after being threatened with dismissal. She raised the matter with her employer who said she should take it up with the security guard's employer which she did. She experienced a negative response from some of her colleagues. During a later internal disciplinary procedure she was subjected to, her company supervisor raised the sexual harassment issue and suggested she was lying about the incident.

The Equality Tribunal made the maximum award of 104

weeks salary (€21,000) to the woman. The case captured the serious nature of sexual harassment and how, even in these extreme circumstances, the response is often one that seeks to trivialise the incident and to isolate the person making the complaint. It highlighted the absence of any adequate policy and procedure on the part of the woman's employer to prevent or address incidents of sexual harassment.

Reasonable Accommodation

Both Acts include one significant positive duty – a requirement on employers and service providers to make reasonable accommodation for people with disabilities. This provision only applies to one ground. However it is an important example of making specific provisions for diversity and acknowledging the need to take account of the practical implications of diversity if equality is to be promoted in the workplace and in the provision of goods and services.

A person selling goods or providing services, a person selling or letting accommodation, educational institutions and registered clubs must do all that is reasonable to accommodate the needs of people with disabilities. This involves providing special treatment or facilities where without these it would be impossible or unduly difficult to avail of the goods, services, accommodation, or education provision. This obligation ceases where the costs involved are more than a nominal cost. This nominal cost exemption might appear to significantly restrict the requirement to make reasonable accommodation. However casework under the Employment Equality Act 1998 demonstrated that nominal cost is not to be interpreted as a fixed sum but that its calculation will depend on such as the size and resources of the organisation involved.

Employers are now required to take appropriate measures to enable a person with disabilities to secure a job, to advance their career or to undertake training unless the measures would impose a disproportionate burden. In assessing disproportionate burden account is taken of the financial and other costs involved, the scale and financial resources of the organisation and the possibility of obtaining public funding or other assistance. The Employment Equality Act 1998 had included a nominal cost exemption in relation to this reasonable accommodation. This was changed under the Equality Act 2004. The new disproportionate burden exemption significantly enhances the potential of these reasonable accommodation provisions to support equality for people with disabilities.

The first successful case under the disability ground in the Employment Equality Act 1998 raised the issue of reasonable accommodation. The complainant worked with a computer component company as a packer. She had epilepsy with the condition well controlled by medication. She had worked in the company for a number of weeks and was told her work performance was very satisfactory and that the company wished to employ her on a permanent basis. However, she was required to have a medical examination. The company terminated her employment on foot of a conversation between the doctor and the company personnel officer informing them of the complainant's epilepsy. The Equality Authority represented the complainant. The Labour Court found that the dismissal was discriminatory and awarded the complainant €19,046.07.

The Labour Court highlighted that the company gave no consideration to providing the complainant with reasonable special facilities to accommodate her needs. The Labour Court pointed out that the company did not consider undertaking any form of safety assessment to assess whether and to what extent the working environment presented a danger to the complainant and how any such dangers could be ameliorated. It further pointed out that the company did not discuss its concerns with the complainant and did not advise her to obtain a second opinion from a neurologist as had been suggested by the doctor.

Victimisation

Both Acts prohibit victimisation. This is an important provision to protect the effective implementation of the legislation. Individual complainants have real fears that by raising the issue of discrimination they will be disadvantaged. It takes courage to bring forward a case and this protection against victimisation is an important support. Victimisation involves the adverse treatment of a person by an employer or service provider because they have made a complaint under the legislation, because they have been a witness in any such proceedings or because they have opposed by lawful means an act that is unlawful under the equality legislation.

In 2000 the Equality Authority supported a claimant making a complaint of victimisation against a Department Store. The complainant made several applications for employment with the respondent. She sought advice from the Equality Authority regarding her allegation that she was being discriminated against by the respondent. She alleged that the respondent was rejecting her application for a job on the ground of disability – because of the fact that she had attended a school for children with learning disabilities. The manager of one of the respondent's branches wrote to her stating 'in view of the untrue and unfounded allegations you have made to the Employment Equality Authority...We are not for the foreseeable future going to accept any application from you for employment in our store or indeed any other branch of (the department store).' The Equality Tribunal found in favour of the complainant and awarded her €12,700. This was the maximum award possible which is a measure of how seriously victimisation is viewed by the Equality Tribunal. The Equality Officer also identified that the success or otherwise of the initial allegation of discrimination was not relevant to the determination of whether or not the complainant was acting in good faith as required by the 1998 Act.

Positive Action

Both Acts allow, but do not require positive action. Positive action is important in the development of a proactive pursuit of equality objectives. Positive action initiatives can target and seek to eliminate significant imbalances between groups in areas such as employment and access to goods and services. Positives action initiatives can make provisions for needs that are specific to groups experiencing inequality. Employers can take steps to ensure full equality in practice between employees on all nine grounds. This definition of positive action in support of full equality in practice is new. It was introduced into the legislation by the Equality Act 2004. It is a definition that goes beyond the concept of equality of opportunity that is the basis for the equality legislation. It provides significant scope for an effective and proactive pursuit of equality objectives in the workplace. Service providers, educational establishments, registered clubs or providers of accommodation can take positive measures to promote equality of opportunity for disadvantaged people or to cater for the special needs of people or a category of people who may require facilities, arrangements, services or assistance because of their circumstances.

Exemptions

Finally, it is important to note that both Acts contain a wide range of exemptions. The Acts are characterised by broad prohibitions on discrimination that are qualified by a range of detailed exemptions. By way of example, under the Employment Equality Acts an employer is not required to employ someone who will not undertake the duties or is not fully competent or capable of doing the job. The Acts are therefore based on the principle of merit and on a focus in workplace decision making on the person's skill and ability rather than irrelevant characteristics. Another example under the Equal Status Acts provides that nothing in the Acts prohibits the taking of any action that is required under statutory provision, court order, any measure or act adopted by the EU and any international treaty posing an obligation on the State. This only covers actions that are mandatory. However it significantly limits the manner in which the Acts cover the public sector as compared to the private sector. It creates a situation where it is possible to legislate in order to discriminate.

EQUALITY LEGISLATION – TRENDS IN EQUALITY AUTHORITY CASEFILES

Employment Equality Acts

In one month alone during 2002 the Labour Court made awards ranging from €5,000 to €15,000 to women who were discriminated against by their employers because they were pregnant. Fifteen thousand euros was awarded to a pregnant woman who was informed by the hotel she worked for that her employment was being terminated by reason of redundancy. This turned out not to be the case, as extra staff were recruited shortly afterwards. In another case a woman was dismissed when she was absent from work due to pregnancy related illness. The restaurant employer took her to have abandoned her job. The Labour Court awarded the woman €12,000 highlighting that a prudent employer acting reasonably would at least have sought to ascertain the true position before treating the complainant's employment as having come to an end. These awards on average amounted to a year's salary of the complainants. This was a significant development and sent a clear message from the Labour Court that pregnancy related discrimination would not be tolerated.

Gender based discrimination is a significant focus in the casefiles of the Equality Authority. Allegations of gender based discrimination made up the highest number of Equality Authority casefiles in 2000, 2001 and 2002. They were the second highest in 2003 and 2004. The allegations of discrimination were predominantly raised by women. They covered in particular issues of pregnancy related discrimination, sexual harassment, promotion and equal pay.

The Equality Authority has discretion in the cases it chooses to support. Choices are made on the basis of criteria established by the Equality Authority. As such these casefiles are not a measure of discrimination experienced within the different grounds. The trends that emerge will reflect the priorities established within the criteria of the Equality Authority. However the trends can also be indicative of a wider pattern of inequality. This trend in Equality Authority casefiles in relation to gender discrimination suggests a persistence to the inequality experienced by women and to the issues of workplace discrimination brought forward by women. This persistence is evident in that gender equality legislation in Ireland dates back to the Anti-Discrimination (Pay) Act 1974 and the Employment Equality Act 1977 and these issues have been a focus in casework for over thirty years. This trend in Equality Authority casefiles in relation to gender discrimination also suggests a significant scale to this experience of discrimination.

The indicative nature of these trends was affirmed in a recent report from the Central Statistics Office, *Women and Men in Ireland, 2004*. This report identified the significant scale and persistence of gender inequality. A number of examples given in the report illustrate this. It reported a significant growth in the employment rate of women from 40.1% in 1994 to 55.8% in 2004. However it highlighted that 'when an adjustment is made for usual hours worked in 2002 (men 41.3 hours and women 31.7 hours) women's hourly earnings were 82.5% of men's.' It found that about 59% of women in the civil service were clerical officers as compared with only 10% of assistant secretaries being women. Around 86% of primary school teachers were women but only 51% of primary school management posts were held by women.[1]

The race ground took over from the gender ground as holding the highest number of Equality Authority casefiles in 2003 and 2004. Equality Authority casefiles on the race ground have grown rapidly in recent years. In 2002 there were fifteen Equality Authority casefiles involving allegations of discrimination on the race ground under the Employment Equality Acts. This represented 7% of the total and was the fourth highest area of casefiles. In 2001 the race ground accounted for 16% of Equality Authority casefiles and 22% in 2002. In 2003 there were 166 Equality Authority casefiles involving allegations of discrimination on the race ground under the Employment Equality Acts. This represented 30% of the total. In 2004 there were 118 such casefiles representing 32% of the total.

The experiences of migrant workers are at the heart of this rapid growth. Migrant workers are a recent phenomenon in terms of holding a significant presence in the Irish workplace. That discrimination should so readily accompany the emergence of this new phenomenon raises issues as to the capacity of organisations and enterprises to prevent discrimination, to accommodate diversity and to promote equality. The casefiles reflect allegations of a harsh exploitation of migrant workers. They include experiences of migrant workers being paid less than their Irish counterparts. In one casefile migrant workers were promised a wage far in excess of what they actually received (which was also less than their Irish counterparts). In another example the migrant workers were paid by the hour while the Irish workers were paid piecework rates. Dismissal is another common experience. In one casefile a migrant worker had an accident at work and was given medical advice not to go back to work until the wound healed. He was told he had to return to his country of origin. In two casefiles migrant workers were threatened with dismissal for attempts to contact a trade union. Excessive working hours is another feature in these casefiles. In one casefile migrant workers were working nearly seventy hours a week and were getting paid for only fifty-five hours a week. They would regularly work seven days a week without getting a break.

In 2005 the Labour Court made an award of €57,900 in respect of an employee who was found to have been discriminated against on the grounds of his disability. The Labour Court was considering two separate claims in relation to the one situation – a claim for discriminatory dismissal and an appeal in relation to an Equality Tribunal finding of discrimination. The case was one of the first to raise issues of mental heath under the disability ground.

The claimant was employed in a specialist capacity for over 14 years with his employer. In April 2002 he was admitted to hospital suffering from a psychiatric illness. He was discharged from hospital in June 2003 and was advised by his psychiatrist that he could return to work preferably on a phased basis. The employer did not allow the claimant to return to work. The complainant was referred to a psychiatrist nominated by the employer and later to an occupational physician. He was eventually allowed to return to work in October 2002. He was given a job description and was told he could no longer deal with clients and that his work would be monitored. The Labour Court accepted that the claimant felt that he was not wanted and that the respondent was intent on making his life difficult. The claimant resigned.

The Labour Court found that the company failed to do all that was reasonable to accommodate the complaint's needs by providing him with special treatment or facilities so as to enable him to return to work on a phased basis. In the Labour Court's view the employer's approach to the complainant on his return to work was not indicative of a caring or sympathetic attitude towards an employee who had been absent from work with a serious psychiatric illness. The Court was satisfied that, having regard to the complainant's undoubted emotional and psychological vulnerability at the time, the conduct of the employer was so unreasonable as to justify the complainant in resigning.

The disability ground has a significant presence in the casefiles of the Equality Authority. In 2004, 16% of these casefiles related to allegations of discrimination on the disability ground. This made up the third largest area of casefiles. The allegation of discrimination related to access to employment, dismissal once the employer became aware of the person's disability and failure to make reasonable accommodation for employees and potential employees with disabilities.

This failure to make reasonable accommodation for people with disabilities is at the heart of most casefiles on the disability ground under the Employment Equality Acts. Reasonable accommodation can involve adapting the workplace or workplace equipment, redesigning working time patterns or task distribution or providing resources for workplace integration. This failure in making reasonable accommodation reflects a significant inflexibility in the workplace that excludes employees with disabilities, an inflexibility that is at odds with the demands of a modern economy if the reluctance to make reasonable accommodation is reflective of wider employment policies, practices and procedures.

In 2001 the Equality Tribunal (ODEI) issued its first finding on the age ground. The Equality Authority took a case against Ryanair for discriminatory advertising. Ryanair had advertised for a director of regulatory affairs in the *Irish Times* in February 2000. The advertisement stated 'we need a young and dynamic professional' and 'the ideal candidate will be young and dynamic'. The word 'young' was found to clearly indicate an intention to exclude applicants who were not young. Ryanair was ordered to pay £8,000 to the Equality Authority, to review its equal opportunities policies and to publish a statement of equal size and prominence as the offending advertisement making a clear commitment to equal opportunities policies.

Ryanair published two statements. One fulfilled the requirements of the Equality Tribunal. The other attacked the Equality Authority stating 'While Ryanair has never discriminated against anyone why has the Equality Authority discriminated against Ryanair and not taken equal action against the *Irish Times*?' This ignored the fact that the *Irish Times* had written to Ryanair agreeing with the Equality Authority that the advertisement was illegal and had sent a memo on the issue to all advertising staff. An intense media debate surrounded this case. One side of the debate sought to attack the finding as political correctness gone astray.[2] This side of the debate ignored the reality that behind the language used a practical exclusion had occurred – there were no applicants over 40 years of age for the job. It exposed a strong strain of ageism – where the capacity, ambition, aspiration and dynamism of an older person is deemed to be assessed purely on the basis of their chronological age.[3] Ageism leads to discrimination when false assumptions and negative stereotypes of older people dictate decision making in relation to their presence and participation in the workplace.

The age ground has consistently been the fourth highest area of Equality Authority casefiles under the Employment Equality Acts. In 2004 these casefiles accounted for 11% of all Equality Authority casefiles under the Acts. These casefiles predominantly related to allegations of discrimination made by older people. These allegations related to access to employment, access to promotion and working conditions in particular.

Equal Status Acts

The Equal Status Acts are still a relatively new area of legislation and trends will take time to fully emerge. One trend that has emerged with extraordinary speed and scale in the casefiles of the Equality Authority relates to allegations of discrimination by licensed premises and by public houses in particular.

In an Irish context the pub is an important arena of social interaction. This is where family and community events are celebrated. It is where people mix and meet friends. It is where people network and do business. Yet allegations of discrimination emerge as a persistent and endemic feature of how publicans manage access to their premises and services. This is clearly a significant source of exclusion for those groups experiencing this discrimination. Equality Authority casefiles

An Ambition for Equality

EMPLOYMENT EQUALITY ACT 1998. CASEWORK ACTIVITY BY
THE EQUALITY AUTHORITY DURING 2004

EEA Rel. Bel	Total / Age	Gender / Disability	M. Status / Race	F. Status / TC	S. Orient / Mixed
Access to Employment	63 / 18	2 / 19	0 / 5	0 / 7	1 / 3
Rel. Bel = 8					
Access to Promotion	19 / 2	8 / 0	0 / 0	0 / 2	0 / 0
Rel. Bel = 7					
Access to Training	7 / 2	2 / 3	0 / 0	0 / 0	0 / 0
Rel. Bel = 0					
Working Conditions	111 / 19	18 / 54	2 / 0	4 / 5	0 / 1
Rel. Bel = 8					
Harassment	22 / 6	3 / 6	1 / 0	0 / 5	0 / 0
Rel. Bel = 1					
Dismissal	58 / 9	13 / 23	0 / 2	1 / 8	0 / 0
Rel. Bel = 2					
Equal Pay	31 / 1	15 / 8	0 / 0	0 / 2	4 / 0
Rel. Bel = 1					
Sexual Harassment	15 / 0	15 / 0	0 / 0	0 / 0	0 / 0
Rel. Bel = 0					
Victimisation	4 / 0	4 / 0	0 / 0	0 / 0	0 / 0
Rel. Bel = 0					
Advertising	7 / 0	4 / 0	0 / 0	0 / 0	0 / 0
Rel. Bel = 3					
Advice	28 / 3	4 / 2	1 / 0	0 / 8	0 / 0
Rel. Bel = 10					
Enforcement Proceedings	1 / 0	0 / 1	0 / 0	0 / 0	0 / 0
Rel. Bel = 0					
Appeal	4 / 0	0 / 2	0 / 0	0 / 0	0 / 0
Rel. Bel = 2					
TOTALS	370 / 60	88 / 118	4 / 7	5 / 37	5 / 4
Rel. Bel = 42					

Note: In each cell the upper value is the top-row heading (Total, Gender, M. Status, F. Status, S. Orient) and the lower value is the bottom-row heading (Age, Disability, Race, TC, Mixed). Rel. Bel totals are given beneath each category name.

The Equality Authority also received requests for assistance in 20 instances in matters which did not come within the ambit of the Employment Equality Act 1998

Note: EEA = Employment Equality Act 1998; M. Status = Marital Status; F. Status = Family Status; S. Orient = Sexual Orientation; Rel. Bel. = Religious Belief; TC = Traveller Community

Source: Annual Report 2004, Equality Authority

under the Equal Status Acts have been dominated by casefiles relating to licensed premises since the introduction of the Acts. The casefiles relate in particular to the Traveller ground but also encompasses the grounds of age, disability, sexual orientation, race, gender, family status and religion.

The use of quotas and 'regulars only' policies emerge in these casefiles as a cover for discrimination. In 2001 a publican admitted operating a quota system whereby no more than five Travellers were served in his pub at any given time. In the case McDonagh vs The Castle Inn the Equality Tribunal found in favour of the claimants and that a quota system for Travellers was totally contrary to the provisions of the Equal Status Act. In the same year another publican admitted that a judgement call was usually made at the door as to whether an individual is admitted and that they usually use the 'regulars only' excuse for refusing entry. In the case of Bernard, Richard and Thomas Joyce vs Liz Delaney's Pub, the Equality Tribunal found in favour of the claimants and found that on the basis of the evidence provided the pub did not enforce a regulars only policy but simply used it as a means to refuse access to individuals they did not want on the premises.

Another case that year that attracted significant public debate was that of Maughan vs The Glimmerman. The claimant was a Traveller who is visually impaired. He came into the pub with his wife who is also visually impaired, his 13-year-old son and his guide dog during the afternoon. He was refused service and the claim was brought forward on the family status, disability and Traveller grounds. The Equality Tribunal found in favour of the claimant on the family status ground.

The publican claimed that the reason the complainant was refused service was because it had a 'no children' policy and the claimant's son kept coming into the pub while the claimant was being served there. The publican claimed that having a 'no children' policy was acting in good faith for the sole purpose of ensuring compliance with the Licensing Acts and therefore was not in breach of the Equal Status Act. The publican also claimed that when parents are consuming alcohol they tend not to supervise their children properly and that its 'no children' policy was designed to prevent disorderly conduct on the premises. In this the publican sought to use two exemptions under the Equal

Status Act – relating to substantial risk of criminal or disorderly conduct or behaviour or damage to property in or around the area where the service is provided and relating to requirements to comply with the Liquor Licensing legislation.

The Equality Tribunal found that having a blanket ban on under-18-year-olds being in pubs with their parents discriminated against parents of children under 18 years old on the family status ground under the Equal Status Act. The finding clarified that this should not be interpreted as meaning that publicans must serve parents when accompanied by their children under 18 in all circumstances. This is because the Licensing Acts require publicans to run orderly houses and to ensure that under-18-year-olds do not consume alcohol on their premises.

This case generated a debate that included much significant misrepresentation about the implications of the case – for example that publicans had to serve anyone accompanied by a child. This was partly due to an error in the original press statement on the case issued by the Equality Authority, but continued long after this had been corrected.

The facts of the case raise significant cultural issues around the place of children in Irish society. They highlight that the model of the Irish pub as a centre for social life is family unfriendly. They demonstrate how people are segregated by generation in the way social life is organised. This was further reinforced in the case of O'Reilly vs The Q Bar where the Equality Tribunal found that a 72-year-old man had been discriminated against on the basis of his age when he was refused access to the Q Bar with his wife, daughter and son-in-law, where they were going to celebrate their anniversary. Older people, children and middle aged adults organise their social lives in isolation from one another. The lack of contact between the generations provides fertile ground for each to hold negative stereotypes and false assumptions about the other. It diminishes the potential for each generation to be enriched by learning from the knowledge, perspectives and experiences of other generations. It limits the solidarity or support that can be offered from one generation to other generations. This cannot be good for society or for each individual generation.

Another trend that is evident in the casefiles of the Equality Authority relates to the provision of educational establishments. Equality Authority casefiles in this area are the second highest after licensed premises under the Equal Status Act. They relate in particular to allegations of discrimination on the Traveller and disability grounds but also cover the grounds of race, gender, religion, age, family status and sexual orientation. They cover a range of issues including allegations of harassment, of discrimination in access to educational establishments and of a failure to make reasonable accommodation for pupils with disabilities.

Few cases have been heard by the Equality Tribunal in relation to the provision of educational establishments. Parents can be reluctant to take the case. Educational establishments have been open to addressing incidents presented to them before a case is taken forward. There can be limited awareness within educational establishments of their obligations under the Acts and an absence of policies and procedures in relation to issues of discrimination, harassment, diversity and equality. In such a situation educational establishment can be open to resolving an issue once they are provided with information on their obligations under the Acts. In one instance the Equality Authority received a query regarding access to a secondary school. The student was put on a waiting list after the school was informed she was a Muslim. The school had been prepared to take a certain number of Muslim children and were effectively operating a quota system. The matter was resolved without litigation. Another case that was similarly resolved involved parents of a student with a disability being required to be present at swimming lessons with their child when their presence was unnecessary and when other parents were not required to be present. A number of cases were resolved that involved access by Traveller children to schools.

A third trend evident in Equality Authority casefiles under the Equal Status Act relates to discrimination in the provision of insurance. This is the third largest area for Equality Authority casefiles under the Equal Status Act. These covered allegations of discrimination on the grounds of age, gender, race, disability, Traveller community and sexual orientation. They covered a range of insurance products including motor, travel and medical insurance. In 2003 the Equality Tribunal made its first finding in relation to an insurance company in

Ross vs Sun Alliance. The Equality Authority represented the complainant.

In 1999 the insurance company that Jim Ross had used for twenty years stopped doing motor insurance. He was 76 at the time, had forty years of accident free driving with seven years No Claims Bonus. He eventually secured insurance at a higher price. However, the price rose again the next year. He sought a new quote from Royal and Sun Alliance. He was refused a quote because of his age due to company policy of not providing insurance to anyone over seventy. The Equality Tribunal found in his favour finding that the complete refusal of a quotation based solely on a person's age without taking account of the individual's particular circumstances was not acceptable. This case highlighted the use of age limits to exclude older people. Age limits are one element of an institutional practice that is ageist – a practice that makes use of a person's age as a basis for excluding them without reference to relevant characteristics or circumstances.

Casefiles relating to the public sector reflect another significant trend in the Equality Authority casefiles under the Equal Status Acts. In 2004, 126 or 25% of all Equality Authority casefiles under the Acts related to allegations of discrimination against the public sector. These covered Government Departments and public sector bodies including in particular the Department of Social and Family Affairs, Health Boards and Local Authorities. The public sector provides services ranging from income support to accommodation to health that are central to people's quality of life. It must therefore be a priority to ensure discrimination does not happen in this sector. The equality legislation could usefully be further developed to ensure that this sector is proactive in taking steps to prevent discrimination and to promote equality.

A number of significant settlements in casefiles relating to the public sector can be identified. In 2002 telephone allowances for people in nursing homes was the subject of a complaint against the Department of Social Community and Family Affairs. The claim involved the grounds of disability and age. It was resolved by the provision of free telephone rental and allowances to nursing home residents over 70 and this was subsequently extended to cover all nursing home residents.

In the same year two asylum seekers with a young baby were allowed to move from direct provision accommodation in a hostel which was unsuitable for their needs after correspondence from the Equality Authority. In 2003 access to suitable accommodation for a Traveller family was refused by the local authority. Tenancy of a four bedroom house was offered after Equality Authority intervention.

A final trend worthy of note in the casefiles of the Equality Authority under the Equal Status Acts relates to golf club membership and the gender ground. The Equal Status Acts make specific provision in relation to registered clubs. A certificate of registration allows clubs to sell alcohol to members and certain visitors. The Equal Status Acts do not prohibit discrimination by registered clubs. A member or applicant for membership cannot seek compensation for discriminatory acts. If a club is deemed to be a discriminatory club by the District Court it can have its certificate of registration suspended for up to 30 days. A subsequent determination would mean no certificate of registration being granted to the club or renewed. A registered club is deemed to be a discriminatory club if it has a rule, policy or practice which discriminates against a member on any of the nine grounds or if someone involved in the management of the club discriminates against a member or applicant in relation to the affairs of the club on any of the nine grounds. A number of exemptions apply to this provision including where the principal purpose of the club is to cater only for the needs of persons of a particular gender, marital status, family status, sexual orientation, religious belief or none, age, disability, nationality or ethnic or national origin or members of the Traveller community. The Equality Authority provided legal advice to members from a number of golf clubs. These related to a range of issues in particular around the manner in which transition from associate to full membership for women was to be achieved, around committee membership and the appointment of officers and around access to the course and other facilities. All were eventually resolved on foot of Equality Authority advice or intervention. The one exception was the issue of membership for women in Portmarnock Golf Club which, as described earlier, eventually involved litigation.

EQUAL STATUS ACT 2000. CASEWORK ACTIVITY BY THE EQUALITY AUTHORITY DURING 2004

ESA	Total	Gender	M. Status	F. Status	S. Orient	Rel. Bel	Age	Disability	Race	TC	Mixed
Prov. Of Services											
Licensed Premises	145	0	0	2	1	0	3	19	3	116	1
Insurance	35	1	0	0	2	0	22	1	4	2	3
Shops	13	1	0	0	0	0	0	2	1	8	1
Social Welfare	20	5	4	0	2	0	1	2	4	1	1
Health Boards	30	1	0	0	0	0	2	12	12	2	1
Local Authorities	26	0	0	0	0	0	0	9	2	13	2
State Dept & Bodies	26	2	0	0	0	0	2	10	9	2	3
Transport	24	1	1	0	0	1	3	16	2	0	1
Banking/Financial	10	1	1	0	0	1	1	6	0	0	0
Other	45	9	1	0	2	2	4	13	9	0	5
Accommodation											
Private	11	2	0	1	0	0	0	1	3	4	0
Public Housing	24	0	0	0	0	0	0	2	4	13	5
Education	74	8	0	0	1	5	1	23	8	18	10
Registered Clubs	11	8	0	0	0	0	1	2	0	0	0
Advice General	15	3	0	1	0	1	1	5	1	1	2
TOTAL	509	41	6	4	8	9	41	123	62	180	35

The Equality Authority also received requests for assistance in 14 instances in matters which did not come within the ambit of the Equal Status Act, 2000

Note: EEA = Employment Equality Act 1998; M. Status = Marital Status; F. Status = Family Status; S. Orient = Sexual Orientation; Rel. Bel. = Religious Belief; TC = Traveller Community

Source: Annual Report 2004, Equality Authority

EQUALITY TRIBUNAL

Redress mechanisms under the equality legislation involve the Equality Tribunal, the Labour Court, the District Court, the Circuit Court and the higher courts. The Equality Tribunal is now established as the first forum for seeking redress for most claims under the equality legislation. Cases on the gender ground under the Employment Equality Acts have the option of going immediately to the Circuit Court. Cases in relation to registered clubs and in relation to licensed premises start in the District Court. The Equality Tribunal in this role as first forum of redress is an important part of the institutional dimension to the strategic framework for action on equality. It was established under the Employment Equality Act 1998. It is a quasi-judicial body with important investigative functions and mediation functions.

This investigative role is important for complainants who are unrepresented or who are represented by groups who do not have legal training. It is particularly important for people with limited capacity to articulate legal arguments, for people without the resources to present a claim and for some people with disabilities. The Acts require the Equality Tribunal to not only hear and decide claims but also to investigate the claim. In traditional adversarial settings the Judge decides a claim based on the evidence and legal arguments presented by both sides. There is no requirement on the judge to investigate further than the evidence made available. The equality officer of the Equality Tribunal plays a much more proactive role in seeking to establish what are the facts and what are the relevant legal issues involved. As such the pursuit or defence of a claim are not wholly dependent on the ability and capacity of either party to marshal the relevant evidence or present complex legal arguments.

The provision of mediation is another important feature of the Equality Tribunal. In practice every claimant and respondent are offered mediation. This is provided where both parties are in agreement in taking up this offer. Mediation can be a flexible, fast and low cost means of dispute resolution which again is not wholly dependent on the capacity and resources of the parties.

The Equality Tribunal also has a range of valuable features in relation to costs and procedures which contrast with traditional court structures. The equality legislation makes no provision for the Equality Tribunal to make an order of costs against either party. Investigations are held in private. This is important for some complainants on the sexual orientation or disability grounds and in cases of sexual harassment or harassment. The Equality Tribunal allows individuals to be represented by community groups or trade unions or trade associations. This broad right of audience is important in a context where the Equality Authority cannot provide legal advice and representation to all complainants. This broad right of audience has been used extensively by both complainants and respondents.

The redress under the equality legislation is a key element in its potential impact. Awards that are effective, proportionate and dissuasive contribute significantly to change in the practice of organisations and to the elimination of discrimination. The equality legislation places some constraints on what is possible in this regard.

Both Acts establish ceilings on the amount of compensation that can be awarded. These ceilings do not apply to cases under the gender ground that are initiated in the Circuit Court. Though the details of these are not available, some significant settlements and at least one judgment have been achieved in gender discrimination cases that were taken to the Circuit Court. There are significant risks in taking such cases in relation to award of costs that would apply in the Circuit Court. However it is an option that demonstrates how ceilings on the amount of compensation that can be awarded could be removed. It is a possibility that could be explored through other mechanisms and applied to all grounds. There are issues with the low level of some of the ceilings on the amount of compensation that can be awarded.

Under the Employment Equality Acts the maximum that a complainant may receive who is not in employment on the date the case is referred is €12,700. The low level of this ceiling makes no allowance for the severity of the discrimination and cannot be seen as dissuasive. This is particularly relevant for many of the new grounds under the Employment Equality Acts that have a limited presence in the workplace and where the major issue is discrimination at the point of interview.

Under the Employment Equality Acts the maximum amount that can be ordered by the Equality Tribunal in cases other than equal pay is calculated on the basis of 104 times the claimant's weekly remuneration. This raises issues where people on low wages bring forward cases of serious discrimination. In the case of sexual harassment described earlier the Equality Tribunal highlighted that it felt constrained by this ceiling in the award it could make.

Under the Equal Status Acts the maximum award that can be made is set at that which can be awarded by the District Court in civil cases which is currently set at €6,350. This does not allow for awards to be effective, proportionate or dissuasive. The low level of this ceiling is at variance with the very fundamental areas of discrimination covered by the Acts including access to education, access to accommodation and access to social services.

Within these ceilings the level of awards made by the Equality Tribunal has also been criticised in relation to cases under the Equal Status Acts involving access to licensed premises.[4] The Legal Review 2003 of the Equality Tribunal sets out awards made in thirty cases involving successful claims of discrimination in relation to access to public houses, hotels, restaurants, off-licences and discos.[5] Twenty three of these were on the Traveller ground, three on the age ground, three on the family status ground and one on the disability ground. There were forty one complainants in these thirty cases. The total awards amounted to €25,553 which is on average only €623 per complainant. This is a level that is far from being effective, dissuasive and proportionate.

The Equality Tribunal does not only make compensation awards: it can also make an order for respondents to take a course of action to address findings made in the cases. This is an important power that has been used to good effect. The Equality Tribunal can also point to key cases, particularly in the employment field where awards made have had a significant deterrent value.

SEEKING TO ENHANCE THE EQUALITY LEGISLATION

Expand the grounds

Section 6 (4) of the Employment Equality Act 1998 states: 'The Minister, shall review the operation of this Act within 2 years of the date of the coming into operation of this section with a view to assessing whether there is a need to add to the discriminatory grounds set out in this section.'[6] As such, on the day of its enactment this legislation was already marked out as unfinished. The Act had sought to be comprehensive in its approach to equality with its coverage of nine grounds – gender, marital status, family status, age, disability, sexual orientation, race, religion and membership of the Traveller community. However, debate during its passage through the Oireachtas had made clear that the Act was far from fully comprehensive. Other grounds were put forward for inclusion. These proposals were responded to by inserting the review clause into the Act.

The draft Constitutional Treaty for the European Union incorporates the EU Charter of Fundamental Rights. Article 21 (1) of the EU Charter of Fundamental Rights provides a clarity as to what a comprehensive approach to equality will need to encompass. It states that 'any discrimination based on any ground such as sex, race, colour, ethnic or social origin, genetic features, language, religion or belief, political or any other opinion, membership of a national minority, property, birth, disability, age or sexual orientation shall be prohibited'.[7] This involves a broad baseline of prohibiting discrimination on any ground and provides an illustrative list that is important in naming the diversity included and establishing the nature of the grounds covered. This is an effective approach that underpins equality legislation that is comprehensive in addressing all forms of discrimination.

The review of the grounds covered by the Act began in 2001 as required by the Act. It has continued up to 2004 with a decision awaited from the Minister for Justice, Equality and Law Reform. It involved submissions from the social partners – in particular Congress, IBEC and the community and voluntary pillar – and organisations such as the Equality Authority. A review seminar was hosted by the Department of Justice, Equality and Law Reform. This allowed for an exchange of views between these organisations. The views put forward by the Equality Authority, Congress and the community and voluntary pillar sought the addition of the grounds of socio-economic status, political opinion, criminal conviction and trade union membership. IBEC was reluctant to have any expansion of the grounds with the view put forward that enterprises needed more time to bed down the original nine grounds. On foot of the review seminar, the Department of Justice, Equality and Law Reform commissioned research by the UCC School of Law on how the four grounds put forward by Congress, the community and voluntary pillar and the Equality Authority were dealt with in other jurisdictions.

The review of the grounds provided an opportunity for the Equality Authority to assess whether there were any issues with the manner in which the existing nine grounds were defined. Three such issues can be identified with the existing grounds under the Employment Equality Act 1998. The first issue related to the age ground. This was defined as covering those between the ages of 18 and 65. This did not reflect the current labour market where people under 18 and over 65 participate in employment. It was an anomaly that the age ground in anti-discrimination legislation was bounded by age limits – themselves so often a source of exclusion for older people. These age limits were removed with the enactment of the Equality Act 2004. The age ground applies to all ages above the maximum age at which a person is statutorily obliged to attend school. Exemptions provide that employers may set a minimum age not exceeding 18 years in recruitment and may set different ages for the retirement of employees.

The ground of gender is not defined to explicitly include transsexual people or the wider transgender community. Change is needed to clarify that transsexual people and the wider transgender community are included under the gender ground and to acknowledge and affirm this diversity within the gender ground. In PvS and Cornwall County Council (1996) EC 1-2143, the Court of Justice held that Article 5 (1) of the original Gender Equal Treatment Directive precludes dismissal of transsexual people for a reason related to gender reassignment. The gender provisions of the Employment Equality Acts now have to be interpreted to afford protection against discrimination to transsexual people in the areas covered by the Acts. Similarly it would appear that the gender provisions of the Equal Status Acts will be interpreted to afford protection to transsexual people even though the gender equal treatment directive does not apply to the areas covered by these Acts. There is a need to amend the definition of the gender ground to reflect this decision of the Court of Justice.

The third issue in relation to the existing nine grounds relates to carers. The family status ground is defined in the Act as meaning responsibility:

(a) as a parent or as a person *in loco parentis* in relation to a person who has not attained the age of 18 years; or
(b) as a parent or the resident primary carer in relation to a person of or over that age with a disability which is of such a nature as to give rise to the need for care or support on a continuing, regular or frequent basis.[8]

The focus on 'resident primary carer' is narrow and excluding. This fails to encompass the broad diversity of caring situations that exist. It does not allow for carers who are non-resident. It means that the importance of shared caring rather than one person as primary carer and the widely differing levels of caring responsibilities are not addressed. There is far more information on the diversity of caring situations since the 2002 Census which included a question on caring for the first time – 'Do you provide regular, unpaid, personal help for a friend or family member with a long term illness, health problem or disability?' Respondents who replied yes to this question were asked to indicate how many hours caring they provided per week from the following categories; 1 to 14 hours, 15 to 28 hours, 29 to 42 hours and 43 or more hours. Fifty-seven per cent of those identifying themselves as carers spend 1–14 hours per week in caring. Over 10% of carers spend 15–28 hours per week in caring and 5.4% spend 29 to 42 hours per week. 27.2% of carers spend 43 hours or more per week. This new information on carers should be reflected in a rewording of the definition of the family status ground.

The review of the grounds provided an opportunity to move towards a more comprehensive approach to combating discrimination and promoting equality under equality legislation. The addition of further grounds would allow all forms of discrimination to be addressed under the legislation. This expansion of the grounds could begin by including the grounds of socio-economic status, criminal conviction, trade union membership and political opinion as recommended by the Equality Authority, Congress and the Community and Voluntary Pillar to social partnership. Socio-economic inequalities are well documented. They cover a broad range of areas including the labour market, health status, education credentials and accommodation situation. There are many factors in the creation and perpetuation of these inequalities. Equality legislation could assist in addressing these inequalities by prohibiting discrimination on the basis of socio-economic status. The Equality Authority recommended the inclusion of a socio-economic status ground highlighting that 'discrimination against an individual on the basis of their socio-economic status can occur where such a person is treated less favourably in relation to:

- job advertising methodology;
- person specification;
- application screening processes;
- interview set-up or process;
- acceptance with the workplace;
- promotion.'[9]

The research carried out on the inclusion of a socio-economic status ground by University College Cork for the Department of Justice, Equality and Law Reform stated that 'it would seem, therefore, that there is a considerable unmet legal need in this area'.[10] It found the most extensive protection against discrimination on the basis of 'social condition' was in Canada where a body of jurisprudence was already developed in Quebec. Social condition is defined in terms of a socially identifiable group that suffers from social or economic disadvantage resulting from poverty, source of income, illiteracy, level of education or any other similar circumstance. In New Zealand a further body of caselaw was identified in relation to discrimination based on employment status. The research suggests that 'the failure to develop more effective anti-discrimination provisions relating to socio-economic status/social origin would seem to be due to a lack of political will and a reluctance to adopt a rights based approach to problems of socio-economic inequality'.

The introduction of a criminal conviction ground would be based on the premise that discrimination against people on the grounds of their criminal record should only be permitted where the offence would be objectively incompatible with the requirements of the job. This ground would have a particular relevance for ex-prisoners given that gaps in their CVs may have to be explained and given the stigma associated with prison. This stigma applies whether the terms of the imprisonment was short or lengthy or for a serious or a less serious offence. It is also relevant given that in Ireland criminal convictions are never 'spent' as happens in other jurisdictions. A concern for the rehabilitation of prisoners is evident in a range of education, training and rehabilitation programmes made available to prisoners. Employment on leaving prison is a key element in this rehabilitation process. Discrimination in employment presents a significant barrier to rehabilitation. The inclusion of a criminal conviction ground to address such discrimination would be consistent with the policy objective of rehabilitating prisoners and would enhance the investment already being made to achieve such an objective. The inclusion of a criminal conviction ground would also be important in ensuring that people do not experience a double punishment for the crime committed – a prison term followed by ongoing discrimination on the basis of the criminal conviction. The Equality Authority recommended the introduction of this new ground highlighting that 'a general anti-discrimination provision would be more effective in helping to rehabilitate those with criminal convictions'.[11]

The research carried out by UCC in relation to this ground found a range of legislative provisions in relation to people with criminal convictions in Australia, Canada, Great Britain, Northern Ireland and the Netherlands. These include a mix of legislation enabling spent conviction and anti-discriminatory legal provisions. Spent conviction includes measures to conceal criminal records. Most anti-discrimination schemes include protection in relation to 'direct and indirect discriminatory provisions'.[12] These schemes cover protection against discrimination in relation to convictions and ancillary circumstances pertaining to convictions. The schemes allow for exceptions related to the inherent requirements of particular jobs. All the schemes cover discrimination in relation to work and many include anti-discrimination provisions in relation to 'accommodation, education, the provision of goods, services, facilities, insurance and superannuation'.[13] The research identifies a tension in the different jurisdictions between the rehabilitative potential of such laws and the priority given to public safety concerns. This tension has led to limitations in the range of offenders who are covered by the legislative provisions in contexts where public safety concerns began to dominate policy priorities.

Protection on the grounds of trade union membership in relation to dismissal is provided for under the Unfair Dismissals Act 1977–93. If it is deemed necessary to protect trade union members from unfair dismissal related to their trade union membership or activities then it must be necessary to provide protection on this ground from other forms of discrimination. The Equality Authority, in recommending the inclusion of a trade union ground, highlighted that 'discrimination may also arise in relation to trade union members who:

- are active in the employment in trade union activities
- engage in industrial action, including secondary action
- refuse to have their conditions of employment governed by 'personal contracts'
- have a history of trade union activity.'[14]

The UCC research found that 'many jurisdictions outlaw employment discrimination based on trade union membership and also discrimination on related grounds such as trade union activity'.[15] The research raises issues in relation to defining the scope of the ground where 'in most jurisdictions the ground covers union membership, non-membership and activities', in relation to making reference to the 'closed shop' in the legislation where a wide variation of approaches were found, and in relation to granting benefits to trade union members where some jurisdictions specifically provide for this.

The Equality Authority recommended the inclusion of a political opinion ground using the formula used in the legislation in Northern Ireland. It stated that 'the core argument for inclusion of this new ground is to secure an equivalence of rights between Ireland and Northern Ireland as committed to in the Belfast Multi-Party Agreement'.[16] An equivalence of rights is important to ensure implementation of the agreement. It is also important in the context of a small island that people are afforded the same protection from discrimination wherever they might be based.

The UCC research found that 'while political opinion is a protected ground across a wide range of jurisdictions (New Zealand, Northern Ireland, most provinces of Canada, most Australian States and the Netherlands) there are relatively few complaints of discrimination based on political opinion'.[17] It found a variety of interpretations of political belief/opinion/convictions across the jurisdictions. It highlights that 'In Northern Ireland the approach has been to characterise political opinions as opinions relating to the conduct of the Government of the State or matters of public policy.'

Transposition of EU Equal Treatment Directives

European Union Equal Treatment Directives have been another important stimulus for change in the equality legislation. The dominant focus in the past for this stimulus has been protection against discrimination on the ground of sex. The Treaty of Rome (1957) included a single article on equality between women and men which related to equal pay (Article 119 EC). This rather limited foundation has given rise to a significant array of gender equality legislation and practice. This focus on anti- discrimination and equality was further developed and expanded in the Amsterdam Treaty (1997). Article 141 EC of this Treaty provided a broad legislative power in relation to women's equality in employment. Article 2 of this Treaty identifies for the first time that equality between men and women is a task of the Community and Article 3 identifies that the Community shall aim to eliminate inequalities, and to promote equality, between men and women in all its activities. Article 13 of this Treaty provides for a general legislative power to tackle a broad range of discrimination based on sex, racial or ethnic origin, religion or belief, disability, age or sexual orientation. This created the necessary conditions for agreement on three new EU Directives – the amended Gender Equal Treatment Directive under Article 141 in 2002,[18] the 'Race' Directive under Article 13 in 2000,[19] and the Framework Employment Directive in 2000.[20]

The amended Gender Equal Treatment Directive prohibits discrimination on the ground of sex in employment, vocational training and promotion and working conditions. It imposes obligations on Member States in relation to gender mainstreaming and provides for enforcement through specialised equality bodies. The 'Race' Directive prohibits discrimination on grounds of race and ethnic origin in access to employment, vocational training, employment and working conditions, involvement in unions and employer organisations, social protection including social security and healthcare, social advantage, education, as well as goods and services including housing. It too requires the establishment of specialised equality bodies. The Framework Employment Directive prohibits discrimination primarily in the employment context – access to employment, self employment and occupations, vocational guidance and training, employment and working conditions. It covers the grounds of disability, age, sexual orientation and religion and belief.

The required transposition of these EU Directives into the Irish equality legislation provided an opportunity to inject new ambition into the equality legislation. The Directives established a minimum standard for equality legislation in the Member States. The development of legislation for their transposition provided a moment to review the equality legislation and to seek improvements that would go beyond what was required by the Directives. The transposition was carried out through the enactment of the Equality Act 2004 which amended the Employment Equality Act 1998 and the Equal Status Act 2000. These Acts are now to be referred to as the Employment Equality Acts 1998 and 2004 and the Equal Status Act 2000 to 2004. The transposition has led to important improvements. However, there is little evidence of ambition beyond what was required by Directives. The transposition might actually be found to fall short of the Directives in some respects. In some instances the Equality Act diminished the provisions of the existing legislation.

The transposition introduced new definitions of indirect discrimination, sexual harassment and harassment and victimisation into the equality legislation. These should improve the context for taking forward cases on these issues. These new definitions apply to all nine grounds under both Acts which enhances coherence between the grounds. The transposition also ensures that the same burden of proof applies to all grounds under both Acts. Prior to this the legislation did not contain any provisions in relation to the burden of proof. Ireland had implemented the Burden of Proof Directive which refers to cases of discrimination based on sex by way of the European Communities (Burden of Proof in Gender Discrimination) Regulation.[21] This provides that 'where in any proceedings facts are established by or on behalf of a person from which it may be presumed that there has been direct or indirect discrimination in relation to him or her, it shall be for the other party concerned to prove the contrary.' The transposition ensures that this approach now applies to all grounds. Prior to this the Equality Tribunal had regularly applied this approach to the burden of proof across all grounds.

Developments in the Employment Equality Act included the removal of upper and lower age limits from the definition of the age ground (although this was accompanied by new exemptions). The Equality Act brought new coherence between the Employment Equality Act and the Equal Status Act by prohibiting discrimination by association and discrimination involving imputation of membership on any of the grounds under both Acts. It improved the provisions on making reasonable accommodation of employees with disabilities in particular by replacing a nominal cost exemption by one based on disproportionate burden on the employer. Unfortunately a similar approach was not introduced under the Equal Status Act. The Equality Act included the self employed, people in partnerships and domestic workers within the scope of the employment equality legislation. However, the employment equality legislation still does not cover the actual recruitment of domestic workers. The Equality Act allowed positive action across all nine grounds and introduced a common and valuable definition of positive action based on ensuring full equality in practice.

Developments specific to the Equal Status Act are less extensive. Previously the Equal Status Act had contained an exemption that permitted a difference of treatment in regard to the provision of accommodation where the premises are a small premises. The definition of small premises was confusing and the transposition of the EU Directives usefully redefined small premises in the exemption.

However, new provisions that actually diminish previous protections under the Equal Status Act were included in the Equal Status Act at the same time as the transposition of the EU Directive. These new provisions introduce two new exemptions in relation to non-nationals. They were enabled by the fact that the 'Race' Directive does not prohibit discrimination against third country nationals and those non-nationals seeking entry into the EU. One of the new exemptions exempts the Minister for Education and Science from a claim of discrimination where she or he 'requires grants to be restricted to persons who are nationals of a member state of the European Union or requires such nationals and other persons to be treated differently in ' relation to the making of grants'.²² This effectively overturned an Equality Tribunal recommendation (Dec 2003-042/043) on this issue. The second new exemption exempts 'any action taken in accordance with any provision or condition made by or under any enactment or made otherwise by a public authority, and governing or arising from the entry to and residence in the State of persons who are not nationals or a category of such persons'.²³

The transposition of the Directives would appear to fall short of the provisions of the Directives in some instances. In this regard it is important to keep in mind that the provisions of the Directives take precedence over the provisions of the equality legislation. One problematic area relates to remedies. The Directives require remedies to be 'effective, proportionate and dissuasive'. The transposition of the Directives did not address this. It failed to change the low level of ceiling on compensation under the Equal Status Act, and on compensation under the Employment Equality Act in relation to access to employment cases. Another problematic area was the failure to give effect to the provisions on gender mainstreaming in the amended Gender Equal Treatment Directive. This Directive requires that 'Member States shall actively take into account the objective of equality between men and women when formulating and implementing laws, regulations and administrative provisions, policies and activities' in areas covered by the Directive and that Members States 'in accordance with national law, collective agreements or practice encourage employers to promote equal treatment for men and women in the workplace in a planned and systematic way'.[24] This could usefully have been given effect to by introducing a statutory duty on the public sector to have due regard to equality in carrying out its functions and by introducing a statutory duty on the private sector to be planned and systematic in their approach to workplace equality. A third problematic area in the transposition of the Directives relates to the failure to expand the scope of the Equal Status Act. The 'Race' Directive applies to categories such as social protection including social security and health, and social advantage that are not mentioned in the Equal Status Act. The Equal Status Act exempts a significant amount of the areas covered by the 'Race' Directive as a result of exempting any Act required by statute. Finally the Equal Status Act does not define services to include the functions of the State, other than services provided by the State, which again reflects a scope narrower than the 'Race' Directive. The transposition fails to address these issues. In particular it fails to expand the definition of services to include functions of the State and to remove the statutory exemption so as to ensure all laws, regulations and administrative provisions contrary to the principle of equal treatment would be void.

This analysis highlights a lack of ambition in seeking to further develop the equality legislation. The transposition of the Directives was a minimalist response to the requirements of the Directives. This analysis also highlights the vulnerability of the equality legislation already in place with the introduction of the new exemptions in relation to non-nationals in the Equal Status Acts. The experience of implementing the equality legislation has also demonstrated the vulnerability of the equality legislation.

WORK UNDER PRESSURE

The Equal Status Acts and their provisions have been particularly subject to pressure. The legislation opens up a new field for anti-discrimination provision. Inevitably this generates tensions as new obligations test the policies, procedures and practices of providers of goods and services, accommodation and educational establishments and registered clubs. The legislation and the political guardianship of the legislation need to be robust in the face of the challenges that will be generated. This robustness has not always been evident and was markedly absent in responding to the challenges posed by the vintners and in the response of the State itself to casework in relation to social welfare provision.

Vintners

The hostility of the vintners' organisations to the Equal Status Act dates back to the original drafting of the legislation. This was responded to with the introduction of two amendments. The first amendment set out that nothing in the Act 'requires a person to provide goods, services or accommodation to a customer if a reasonable individual, having the knowledge and experience of the provider, would form the belief on grounds other than discriminatory grounds that the provision of service or accommodation to the customer would produce a substantial risk of criminal or disorderly conduct or behaviour or damage to property in or around the area where the service is provided'.[25] The exemption would appear to be unnecessary in a context where the belief is formed 'on grounds other than discriminatory grounds'. However, it has the effect of placing an onus on complainants in cases where the exemption is used as a defence to establish their good character and that of their family and friends.

The second amendment exempted 'action taken in good faith by or on behalf of a licence holder for the sole purpose of ensuring compliance with the provisions of the Licensing Acts 1833 to 1999'.[26] There is already an exemption in relation to Acts required by another statute which makes this amendment unnecessary. The words 'in good faith' add the further factor of intent – the person could act in good faith and be wrong. This factor of intent is not referred to in any other provisions in the equality legislation. These amendments created a context where the vintnera' organisation felt able to approach the Equality Authority in 2000 prior to enactment of the Equal Status Act to seek the preparation of a Code of Practice on access to pubs, hotels, nightclubs and restaurants.

By 2002 Tadhg O'Sullivan of the Vintners' Federation of Ireland was being quoted in the *Irish Examiner*. 'Instead of equality we now have special status for some members in society who are supported actively by the Equality Authority under the Equal Status Act. The decisions that are being handed down are ludicrous...It is state sponsored extortion, state sponsored blackmail.' He went on: 'The difficulties we experience with Travellers using the Equal Status Act are huge. It is being used and abused as a tool for blackmail and extortion – it is a gravy train.' He said the VFI would not cooperate with the drafting of a code of practice, stating: 'We cannot engage with an agency in practices that are discriminating against publicans.'[27] He failed to acknowledge that the low ceiling on compensation, very low awards, limited success rate and long delays in the hearing of cases meant that taking a case was far from a money making venture. Frank Fell of the Licensed Vintners Association was not far behind stating the same year that 'we see this thing as a total racket. It has turned itself into another industry and it is just another way of shutting down publicans'.[28]

The Vintners ran an advertising campaign in regional print media seeking to undermine the Equal Status Act. They lobbied extensively against the Act at a political level. The May 2002 Conference of the Vintners' Federation of Ireland carried a motion expressing concern at the manner in which the Equal Status Act was being implemented, condemning Equality Tribunal decisions as unreasonable and demanding the strongest possible action by the Vintners' Federation of Ireland to protect its members. An *Irish Times* editorial following the conference, referring to this and other motions, stated that 'in normal circumstances the behaviour of the VFI would be regarded as outrageous but publicans have dictated their own terms of behaviour to governments for such a long time that their bullying approach is taken for granted'.[29]

During the summer months of 2002 the Vintners' Federation of Ireland threatened a national ban on Traveller access to pubs. A local ban was said to be already in place in Westport. The situation was defused through a series of meetings between Minister of State Willie O'Dea, Vintners' organisations and Traveller organisations. On foot of these the Vintners' organisations agreed to reinitiate work with the Equality Authority on the Code of Practice. They never did, despite an invitation to do so. The Equality Authority made a briefing note available to the Minister of State that highlighted that the Equal Status Act makes it an offence for a person to procure or attempt to procure another person to engage in prohibited conduct and that this section of the Act could be applied to those involved in seeking to have a blanket ban on serving Travellers imposed by publicans.

These actions by the Vintners' organisations were a response to the high levels of complaints being made against publicans under the Equal Status Act in particular by members of the Traveller Community. At the time of the proposed ban current Equality Authority casefiles under the Equal Status Act numbered 542. Of these, 315 related to allegations of refusal to serve by pubs, nightclubs and hotels. These covered the ground of gender (1), family status (6), sexual orientation (3), age (13), disability (14) race (9) and membership of the Traveller community (262). The response to what the Equality Authority identified as 'persistent, sustained and endemic discrimination and a profound reluctance to make this arena of social interaction more inclusive'[30] was to define the legislation and its institutions as the problem. At no stage did the Vintners take responsibility for their own practice and procedures and for how discrimination appeared to be integral to the manner in which they managed what is a complex and challenging business.

The response of Government began on foot of the widespread debate that followed the Equality Tribunal finding in the case of Maughan vs The Glimmerman which is described earlier in this chapter. In March 2002 Minister for Justice Equality and Law Reform John O'Donoghue announced that he was going to amend the Equal Status Act to make clear that decisions taken in good faith by licensees not to allow children in, shall not constitute discrimination. This decision was criticised by the Equality Authority.[31] The Equality Authority suggested that any such change would be better introduced on the basis of a body of caselaw and an analytical review of this caselaw. It pointed out that amendments made as a result of pressure and controversy set a dangerous precedent for the future integrity of the legislation.

At the same time the Minister decided to extend the terms of reference of the Commission on Liquor Licensing to examine the rights of licence holders to refuse admission. The Equality Authority pointed out that the Commission was made up predominantly of vintner, hotelier and restaurant organisations without equality or human rights interests present.[32] The focus in the new terms of reference for the Commission on the right of vintners to refuse ignored the need for a focus on the responsibilities of licence holders. It is not insignificant that the Equality Authority holds the statutory function to keep the Equal Status Act under review and to make recommendations for change to the Minister and yet was not asked to provide any such advice to the Minister.

The Commission on Liquor Licensing reported in December 2002. It made recommendations in relation to restricting children in licensed premises and refusing admission to groups of persons where there is a danger of disorderly conduct. In an extraordinary departure from its terms of reference it included a chapter on 'Issues Arising in relation to Equality Infrastructure'. This chapter was highly and unfairly critical of the Equality Tribunal – without affording any right of reply to the Equality Tribunal. It examined the background and training of equality officers stating: 'It is therefore striking that a legal qualification is not considered necessary even though equality officers have a jurisdiction equivalent to that of a District Court judge and may order a person to take a specified course of action.'[33] It highlighted that 'the licensed trade supports the establishment of a more representative tribunal to replace the ODEI' and stated 'The Commission considers that some adjustment to (Equality Tribunal) structures may yet prove necessary, in particular the establishment of a panel selected by service providers and minority groups covered by the equality legislation.' It also stated that 'The Commission in general advocates recourse to the District Court when dealing with all licensing issues.' Finally, it recommended that 'an independent study of procedural issues be undertaken to ensure fairness to complainants and respondents alike'.

The Government responded positively to the suggestion by the Commission in relation to recourse to the District Court. The Minister for Justice, Equality and Law Reform, Michael McDowell TD, introduced the Intoxicating Liquor Act 2003 to the Dáil. This gave discretion to licence holders to exclude children from licensed premises at any time and required them to exclude those under 18 years of age after 9 p.m. It allowed licence holders to set an age over 18 for the sale of alcohol. Most significantly it transferred jurisdiction from the Equality Tribunal to the District Court for cases of discrimination in relation to licensed premises. An editorial in the *Irish Examiner* stated: 'Worrying signs of creeping authoritarianism, mixed with a disregard for the interests of minority groups, are manifest in the proposal by Justice Minister Michael McDowell to radically change the way this country's equality legislation operates.'[34]

The outcome of this change has been a massive reduction in cases in relation to discrimination by publicans. This reduction reflects the important role played by the Equality Tribunal in the effective implementation of equality legislation. The District Court does not have the investigative role of the Equality Tribunal, it cannot offer mediation, it does not have the same broad right of audience afforded by the Equality Tribunal. The District Court also holds the risk of financial awards. The intoxicating liquor legislation could have addressed these issues which are in effect barriers to accessibility. The District Court could have been allowed to request the Equality Tribunal to nominate an equality officer to investigate and prepare a report on any question specified by the District Court. The District Court could have been allowed to refer a case to the Equality Tribunal for mediation. The new legislation could have addressed issues of costs and rights of audience. None of these steps were taken. The only positive element in this change in the legislation was the provision of additional types of redress such as an order for temporary closure of the premises and to allow for an objection in writing against an application of a renewal of a licence to which the Court would have regard. These could act as real deterrents to discrimination if the legislation had addressed the barriers to access to the District Court identified above.

The Intoxicating Liquor Act 2003 also failed to adequately transpose the powers and functions of the Equality Authority. The new Act allowed the Equality Authority to provide assistance at its discretion in cases relating to discrimination under the Act. However, the functions of the Equality Authority to provide information on the Act, to prepare codes of practice on matters covered by the Act and to conduct equality reviews or inquiries in relation to licensed premises were not transposed. This has left the Equality Authority with a very limited role in addressing issues of discrimination by licensed premises. This has also contributed to the reduction of cases in this area.

Social Welfare Provision

A further limitation on the Equal Status Act resulted from the successful settlement of a case against the Department of Social and Family Affairs. The case was taken on the sexual orientation ground and supported by the Equality Authority. It involved a gay man who was eligible for a free travel pass. The Department of Social and Family Affairs refused to issue a travel pass to the cohabiting partner of the gay man. Under the free travel scheme a person aged 66 or over who is married or cohabiting is entitled to a free travel pass allowing a spouse or partner to accompany him or her on public transport. In September 2003 the Department accepted that the scheme, insofar as it did not extend equal benefits to same sex and opposite sex cohabiting couples, ran counter to the Equal Status Act. Both men received compensation and the application for a travel pass was accepted.

By March 2004 the Department of Social and Family Affairs was introducing an amendment under the Social Welfare (Miscellaneous) Provisions Bill to limit the definition of spouse and couple to a married couple and to a cohabiting couple of the opposite sex. This amendment related to both statutory and non-statutory schemes. The Department was in effect legislating to discriminate in the aftermath of the settlement reached. This amendment takes advantage of the exemption in the Equal Status Act that exempts any action required by statute from the provisions of the legislation. Once again the Equal Status Act was found to be a work under pressure.

Grounds

The equality legislation seeks to be comprehensive in its multi-ground approach. It is impressive and groundbreaking in this regard with its coverage of nine different grounds. The review process under the Employment Equality Act has established the case to expand this coverage with the inclusion of the grounds of socio-economic status, criminal conviction, trade union membership and political opinion. The incorporation of the Charter of Fundamental Rights into the draft constitutional treaty for the European Union opens a broader range of grounds and establishes a valuable ambition to tackle any discrimination based on any ground. The search to be comprehensive in the approach of the equality legislation is important. It ensures that hierarchies are not imposed between different experiences of discrimination and situations of inequality. All forms of discrimination are usefully deemed to be unacceptable in a truly comprehensive approach. This could start by including the four new grounds already proposed. It would be further developed by adopting the approach of the Charter of Fundamental Rights in covering all forms of discrimination. This would address the full range of identities within a society alongside the different statuses or situations of particular groups that experience inequality.

EU Directives

The EU 'Race' Directive requires an expansion of the scope of the Equal Status Act in relation to the grounds covered by the Directive such that the definition of services would include the functions of the State or the exercise of its powers by the State. The 'Race' Directive, the Framework Employment Directive and the amended Gender Equal Treatment Directive require a review and amendment or removal of many of the exemptions in the equality legislation in particular the exemption under the Equal Status Act for any act required by another statute. These Directives require an approach to remedies that would be effective, proportionate and persuasive. The amendments made in the equality legislation as part of seeking to transpose the EU Directives have not been a sufficient response to their requirements. Further amendments are necessary to fully reflect the obligations established by these EU Directives.

Statutory Duty

Developments in equality legislation in other jurisdictions suggest the need to consider not only a progressive improvement of the equality legislation but also a qualitative evolution of the legislation. Positive duties on the public and private sectors have emerged as central to the new generation of equality legislation in a number of jurisdictions. Such statutory duties are provided for in Norway, Northern Ireland, Wales and Britain for example.

The Norwegian Gender Equality Act 1978 prohibited any form of discrimination on the gender ground. It required the public sector to promote equality. The Norwegian Ombud institution has used the Act 'to examine the work of all kinds of public decision makers or authorities'.[35] The Ombud has done this by opinions on policy proposals prepared on the basis of hearings, by handling complaints about public sector bodies and by suggesting and initiating change where the Ombud identified practice or proposals that work against gender equality. The revised Gender Equality Act was passed through the Stortinget in 2002. It includes a new section, 'The Duty to Promote Gender Equality'. Public authorities are required to work actively and systematically to promote gender equality in all sectors of society. Employers in both the public and private sectors have a corresponding duty as employers within their organisation. All private sector enterprises have a statutory duty to include information on gender equality in their annual report. This report has to provide gender based statistics on a range of issues including recruitment, promotion, pay and use of parental leave. The report must identify measures taken or planned in response to the duty to work actively and systematically to promote gender equality. The annual report of enterprises is controlled by a public register which now checks for the inclusion of this material on gender equality. Public Authorities and public enterprises that are not obliged to prepare annual reports must provide similar information as part of their annual budgets. This is controlled by the Ministry responsible for these budgets. The Ombud for gender equality has responsibility for controlling and following up on the quality of these reports.

Section 75 of the Northern Ireland Act 1998 requires public authorities to have due regard to the need to promote equality of opportunity in carrying out their functions. This covers the grounds of religious belief, political opinion, racial group, age, marital status, sexual orientation, gender, disability and people with or without dependents. Public authorities are required to produce an Equality Scheme setting out how they propose to fulfil this statutory duty. This must be submitted to the Equality Commission for Northern Ireland and conform to guidelines that have been published with the approval of the Secretary of State. The scheme must include the arrangements for assessing and consulting on the impact on equality of opportunity of policies adopted or proposed to be adopted. The Equality Commission for Northern Ireland has published Practical Guidance on Equality Impact Assessments. Such assessments must be applied to those policies or legislative developments which are likely to have the greatest impact on equality of opportunity.

The Government of Wales Act 1998 requires the Welsh National Assembly to make appropriate arrangements with a view to securing that its functions are exercised with due regard to the principle that there should be equality of opportunity for all people. This is unique in being directed at all social groupings. Under the Act the National Assembly may be subject to judicial review if it is considered to have failed to comply with the provisions of the equality duty.

In Britain the Race Relations Amendment Act 2000 sought to address the issue of institutional discrimination. This was on foot of recommendations made in the report of the Lawrence

Inquiry. This was set up to examine the handling of the racist murder of a young Black teenager, Stephen Lawrence, in South London. This Act places a statutory duty on approximately 40,000 listed public authorities to promote race equality. They are required, in carrying out their function, to have due regard to the elimination of unlawful discrimination, the promotion of equality of opportunity and the promotion of good 'race relations' between different 'racial groups'. This general duty is accompanied by specific duties tailored to specific sectors. For example, specific duties apply to the main public services such as local government, health bodies, central Government Departments, the police and criminal justice agencies to produce Race Equality Schemes. These schemes are in effect a three year strategy and an action plan for 'race' equality. The scheme must address the need to assess and consult on the impact of future policies on 'race' equality. A similar statutory duty has been developed on the disability ground and is now promised for the gender ground in Britain.

The Employment Equality Acts and the Equal Status Acts are predominantly based on an individual enforcement model. They allow individuals to bring civil actions challenging discrimination. However it is important to acknowledge that they do go beyond the individual enforcement model in some of the powers given to the Equality Authority. These include the preparation of codes of practices, conducting inquiries and equality reviews and actions plans, and instituting proceedings without a claimant where there is a general practice of discrimination.

Gains have been achieved through an individual enforcement model. Individuals experiencing discrimination have secured change in their situation and experience. Legal precedents have been set. A culture of enforcement has created a context for new institutional practice. Individual cases have provided a stimulus and a focus for debate at national and local level on equality issues. However, it is clear that the individual enforcement model on its own provides only a limited response to the persistence of discrimination and inequality. This has resulted in the development in other jurisdictions of a new generation of equality legislation that involves statutory duties to promote equality alongside an individual enforcement model.

The individual enforcement model has a number of significant limitations.[36] It is dependent on the willingness, courage, capacity and resources of an individual to bring forward a case. It is comparator based with its understanding of discrimination in terms of less favourable treatment. It cannot deal with situations where there is no comparator or where the treatment is consistent but consistently poor. It is based on retrospective fault finding. This creates an adversarial context and stimulates defensive rather than generous reactions.

A statutory duty has a capacity to secure an institutional practice that prevents discrimination happening. It has a capacity to secure benefit not only to individuals that allege discrimination but to groups or communities that experience inequality. It stimulates a proactive, planned and systematic approach to equality that has a capacity to achieve benefits for the organisation and a diversity of employees and customers.

Irish equality legislation should include statutory duties to promote equality if it is to fully make its contribution within a strategic framework for action on equality to a more equal society. It is important that the model for a statutory duty would draw on the learning and practice of other jurisdictions. This suggests that a statutory duty should:

• introduce equality mainstreaming into the public sector by requiring designated bodies to have due regard to equality in carrying out their functions. This would ensure that the policy objectives established in equality legislation would be supported by legislative developments, policy making and programme design across the full public sector. This coherence of effort will greatly enhance the impact made on current inequalities;

• introduce equality mainstreaming into the private sector by requiring a planned and systematic approach to equality through the preparation of enterprise level equality action plans. This would ensure that the private sector matches the efforts of the public sector in promoting equality. It would allow approaches to promoting equality to be tailored to current business systems within the private sector. It would also allow a diversity of approaches within the private sector to reflect differences in size and nature of organisations in the sector;

- be based on clear objectives to realise full equality in practice for all groups covered by the equality legislation and to address material inequalities experienced by these groups. These objectives would establish the vision for a more equal society to be supported by the legislation. They would reflect the new definition of positive action based on full equality in practice introduced into the equality legislation with the transposition of the EU Equal Treatment Directives;
- create a role for the Equality Authority as the independent specialised equality body in establishing, keeping under review and monitoring the approaches used in implementing this statutory duty. This would ensure common standards across the public sector and across the private sector. It would allow an independent and expert perspective to shape and inform the implementation of a statutory duty;
- impose effective, proportionate and dissuasive sanctions where there is a failure to implement the statutory duty adequately and appropriately. Sanctions are important to sustaining approaches required by a statutory duty into the long term;
- be based on a requirement that implementation of the statutory duty would involve the participation of those who experience inequality and their organisations. This participation provides valuable information for decision makers. It supports an implementation of the statutory duty in a manner that is evidence based.

A statutory duty to promote equality developed in such manner will be key in addressing and eliminating the institutional patterns of discrimination and the failures to take account of needs specific to particular groups that underpin persistent inequalities. It will be key in stimulating a coherent approach to greater equality across all sectors in society.

Reasonable Accommodation

This new generation of equality legislation could include a further evolution of some provisions already in the legislation. There is already a positive duty on employers and service providers to make reasonable accommodation for people with disabilities. This provision is already evolving beyond the disability ground. This is evident in the protection afforded to pregnant women and in precedent described earlier in this chapter which was established by the Labour Court on the race ground in relation to the cultural and linguistic diversity of migrant workers in the workplace. It is a duty that could usefully be extended across all grounds covered by the equality legislation. This would acknowledge difference and the need for institutional policy and practice to make adjustments for the practical implications of difference across the nine grounds. A broad duty to reasonably accommodate would create a dialogue between employers or service providers and their employees or customers from across the nine grounds that would assist in identifying the needs of those employers or customers and how best to meet these. This would enhance the contribution of a diversity of employees to business success while also improving their situation and experience. It would enhance quality customer service and the benefits to business from this while also enhancing the relevance and impact of services provided to a diversity of customers.

Positive Action

There is already a focus on positive action in the equality legislation. This is allowed under both Acts across all nine grounds. Requirements in relation to positive action that would address significant imbalances in the situation of groups experiencing inequality could usefully be developed in the legislation. This would overcome the experience where the voluntary nature of current provisions and the uncertainty around their scope has meant they are not deployed adequately or to sufficient effect. Requirements on employers and service providers to take positive action where significant imbalances in equality outcomes are identified would underpin and ensure a targeting of resources and of initiatives to address and eliminate current inequalities.

The operation of fair employment legislation and its effective use of positive action to address considerable and persistent labour market disadvantage for Catholic people in Northern Ireland provides a valuable example in this regard.[37] This legislation dates back to 1976. However the reform of this legislation in 1989 emphasised a focus on positive action. It introduced compulsory monitoring of employees on the basis of religion by employers and established a range of actions permitted within affirmative action agreements. Affirmative action permitted steps short of the use of quotas. It does include setting goals and targets for improving employment patterns of an employer based on a comparison between the existing patterns and the profile of the relevant geographical catchment area. The Fair Employment Commission had powers to conduct investigations of organisations and conclude affirmative action agreements with them. One further development in this regard was the introduction of a required 50:50 Protestant/Catholic recruitment ratio into the new Police Service of Northern Ireland on foot of the Patten Report. These processes have significantly reduced labour market disadvantage for Catholic people in Northern Ireland.[38] They underpin the case for developing requirements in relation to positive action in Irish equality legislation where inequalities in the situation of particular groups are significant and persistent.

NOTES

1. *Women and Men in Ireland 2004*, Central Statistics Office, Stationery Office (Dublin) 2004
2. O'Connor, B. in *Sunday Independent* 11th February 2001 and Collins, L. in *Sunday Independent* 18th February 2001, for example
3. Myers, K. in *Irish Times* 14th February 2001 and O'Connor, B. in *Sunday Independent* 11th February 2001, for example
4. *Annual Report 2003*, Equality Authority (Dublin) 2004
5. *Legal Review 2003*, Equality Tribunal (Dublin) 2004
6. *Employment Equality Act 1998*, Stationery Office (Dublin) 1998
7. *EU Charter of Fundamental Rights*, Official Journal C 364/01 December 2001
8. *Employment Equality Act 1998*, Stationery Office (Dublin) 1998
9. *Review of Discriminatory Grounds Covered by the Employment Equality Act 1998*, An Equality Authority Position, Equality Authority (Dublin) 2001
10. Kilcummins, McClean, McDonagh, Mulally and Whelan, *Extending the Scope of Employment Equality Legislation: Comparative Perspectives on the Prohibited Grounds of Discrimination*, Report commissioned by the Department of Justice Equality and Law Reform, University College Cork, Stationery Office (Dublin) 2004

11. *Review of Discriminatory Grounds Covered by the Employment Equality Act 1998*, An Equality Authority Position, Equality Authority (Dublin) 2001
12. Kilcummins, McClean, McDonagh, Mulally and Whelan, *Extending the Scope of Employment Equality Legislation: Comparative Perspectives on the Prohibited Grounds of Discrimination*, Report commissioned by the Department of Justice Equality and Law Reform, University College Cork, Stationery Office (Dublin) 2004
13. Kilcummins, McClean, McDonagh, Mulally and Whelan, *Extending the Scope of Employment Equality Legislation: Comparative Perspectives on the Prohibited Grounds of Discrimination*, Report commissioned by the Department of Justice Equality and Law Reform, University College Cork, Stationery Office (Dublin) 2004
14. *Review of Discriminatory Grounds Covered by the Employment Equality Act 1998*, An Equality Authority Position, Equality Authority (Dublin) 2001
15. Kilcummins, McClean, McDonagh, Mulally and Whelan, *Extending the Scope of Employment Equality Legislation: Comparative Perspectives on the Prohibited Grounds of Discrimination*, Report commissioned by the Department of Justice Equality and Law Reform, University College Cork, Stationery Office (Dublin) 2004
16. *Review of Discriminatory Grounds Covered by the Employment Equality Act 1998*, An Equality Authority Position, Equality Authority (Dublin) 2001
17. Kilcummins, McClean, McDonagh, Mulally and Whelan, *Extending the Scope of Employment Equality Legislation: Comparative Perspectives on the Prohibited Grounds of Discrimination*, Report commissioned by the Department of Justice Equality and Law Reform, University College Cork, Stationery Office (Dublin) 2004
18. Parliament and Council Directive 2002/73/EC of 23rd September 2002 amending Council Directive 76/207/EC on the implementation of the principle of equal treatment for men and women as regards access to employment, vocational training and promotion and working conditions (2002) OJ L 180/22
19. Council Directive 2000/43/EC of 29th June 2000 implementing the principle of equal treatment between persons irrespective of racial or ethnic origin (2000) OJ L 180/22
20. Council Directive 2000/78/EC of 27th November 2000 establishing a general framework for equal treatment in employment and occupation (2000) OJ L 303/16
21. Council Directive 97/80/EC on the Burden of Proof in cases of Discrimination based on Sex (1998) OJ L 14
22. Equality Act 2004, The Stationery Office (Dublin) 2004
23. Equality Act 2004, The Stationery Office (Dublin) 2004
24. Parliament and Council Directive 2002/73/EC of 23rd September 2002 amending Council Directive 76/207/EC on the implementation of the principle of equal treatment for men and women as regards access to

employment, vocational training and promotion and working conditions (2002) OJ L 180/22

25. Equal Status Act 2000, The Stationery Office (Dublin) 2000
26. Equal Status Act 2000, The Stationery Office (Dublin) 2000
27. Fionnuala Quinlan, *Irish Examiner*, Monday, 18th March 2002
28. Rachel Andrews, *Sunday Tribune*, 30th June 2002
29. *Irish Times*, 25th May 2002
30. *Annual Report 2001*, Equality Authority (Dublin) 2002
31. Carol Coulter, *Irish Times*, 28th March 2002
32. Carol Coulter, *Irish Times*, 28th March 2002
33. *Report on Admission and Service in Licensed Premises*, Commission on Liquor Licensing, The Stationery Office (Dublin) December 2002
34. *Irish Examiner*, 12th June 2003
35. Mile, K., in *Mainstreaming Equality: Models for a Statutory Duty*, Equality Authority (Dublin) 2003
36. Barry, E., 'Different Hierarchies – Enforcing Equality Law' in *Equality in Diversity: The New Equality Directive*, Edited by Cathryn Costelloe and Eilis Barry, Irish Centre for European Law and Equality Authority (Dublin) 2003
37. Osborne, B. and Shuttleworth, E. (eds), *Fair Employment in Northern Ireland – A Generation On*, Blackstaff Press (Belfast) 2004
38. Osborne, B. and Shuttleworth, E. (eds), *Fair Employment in Northern Ireland – A Generation On*, Blackstaff Press (Belfast) 2004

Chapter Four

A Dual Strategy

TARGETING AND MAINSTREAMING

Targeting and mainstreaming are two further dimensions that are central to the strategic framework for action on equality. They fit alongside institutions and legislation as the central dimensions to this strategic framework. Targeting and mainstreaming are distinct dimensions. However, they need to be closely linked if they are to be effective in contributing to the achievement of equality objectives.

As set out in Chapter One equality objectives focus on access to resources (economic equality), access to decision making (political equality), access to status and a valuing of diversity (cultural equality), and access to relationships of love, care and solidarity (caring equality). Targeting involves directing resources, policies and programmes at specific groups experiencing inequality with a view to furthering these equality objectives for those groups. Targeting is needed to address situations of inequality experienced by groups as a result of a history of discrimination and exclusion. It is needed to address and respond to needs that are specific to particular groups that currently experience inequality.

A transfer of resources to those groups experiencing inequality can be achieved through carefully targeted initiatives. Enhanced access to resources for groups experiencing inequality is a core equality objective. Targeted initiatives can involve budgetary allocations that make finance or other resources available to meet the needs of and to promote equality for these different groups. It is only in this way that the impact of historical and current experiences of discrimination and exclusion can be effectively addressed. This contribution is explored in this chapter in relation to the National Disability Strategy.

Empowerment and capacity building for groups experiencing inequality can be supported by initiatives targeted on these groups. Participation in decision making by groups experiencing inequality is a core equality objective. Targeted initiatives can involve programmes to support the development of organisations within groups experiencing inequality and the participation by these organisations in decision making that impacts on these groups. This equality objective of participation in decision making must be accompanied by a commitment to effective participation and to developing the ability of groups to engage as equal partners in the decision-making process. Targeted initiatives in this area can invest in training and personal development for members of these groups. This contribution is explored in this chapter in relation to the National Anti-Poverty Networks Programme and to the Community Development Programme.

Enhanced access to relationships of love, care, and solidarity for groups experiencing inequality is a core equality objective. Targeted initiatives have a particular contribution to make in creating a context where members of these groups have the necessary access to relationships of care. Targeted initiatives can support an infrastructure of caring services or can involve policy development to support people to play caring roles. This contribution is explored in this chapter in relation to parental leave legislation.

Targeted initiatives contribute to ensuring that needs specific to the identity, experience or situation of particular groups are adequately and appropriately met. Access to status and a valuing of diversity is a core equality objective. Diversity has practical implications. Different identities, experiences and situations of particular groups mean that there are needs specific to these groups. The development and implementation of policies and programmes to meet these needs necessarily involves targeted initiatives where needs are specific to the group. This contribution of targeted initiatives is explored in this chapter in relation to Traveller accommodation.

Mainstreaming seeks to promote equality through all key

policies, programmes and practices in both the public and the private sectors. It involves designing these policies, programmes and practices so that they take account of diversity and contribute to equality objectives being pursued. In this way, whatever the primary objective or focus of these policies, programmes and practices, they can be coherent with and, where possible, contribute to equality objectives. Mainstreaming involves decision makers including equality as one further factor in the decisions they make. It also involves a participation by those groups experiencing inequality within the decision-making process. This participation provides a necessary source of knowledge and information for equality to be a factor in key decision making.

Mainstreaming is explored in this chapter in terms of gender mainstreaming, equality impact assessments, integrated poverty and equality proofing, which all relate to the public sector, and in terms of employment equality reviews in the private sector. Gender mainstreaming has been developed to ensure the National Development Plan contributes to equality between women and men. Equality impact assessments were applied by the City and County Development Boards in the preparation of their ten year strategy plans to ensure that these plans contributed to equality for groups across the nine grounds. Integrated equality and poverty proofing has been applied in two policy initiatives to support their focus on poverty and equality issues. Employment equality reviews enable employers to bring a focus on equality and diversity into their workplace policies, procedures and practices. These reviews have been piloted by the Equality Authority with private sector and public sector employers.

Targeting and mainstreaming need to be integrated to form part of a dual strategy to promote equality. Segregation and marginalisation can result for groups experiencing inequality where targeted initiatives are the sole response to inequality. General policies, programmes and practice do not accommodate diversity and groups end up depending on separate policies, programmes and practice to meet their needs. Inequalities can persist for groups experiencing inequality where mainstreaming is the sole response to inequality. Mainstreaming is focused on the future impact of policies, programmes and practices and will not necessarily redress current imbalances and inequalities between groups. A dual strategy means that some targeted initiatives will be taken to support the capacity of mainstream institutions and organisations to take account of diversity and to promote equality. It means that mainstreaming will stimulate decision makers to put in place targeted initiatives where inequalities are identified that will not be addressed by general policies, programmes or practices.

TARGETING TO ENHANCE ACCESS TO RESOURCES

The National Disability Strategy announced in 2004 provides an example of a targeted initiative concerned with the transfer of resources to people with disabilities. It sought to combine new investment, new legislation and new policy and practice within a strategy targeting inequality and exclusion among people with disabilities. Significant new investment was committed to the provision of services to people with disabilities. New administrative procedures were required by some Government Departments to plan for greater equality and inclusion for people with disabilities. However, the legislation – the Disability Bill 2004 and the Comhairle (Amendment) Bill 2004 – failed to mark a new departure in targeted initiatives in that it does not provide an unequivocal rights basis for people with disabilities to new resources and services.

A rights based approach to the allocation of resources – whether financial resources or in services provided – would ringfence particular resources to meet the needs of the specific group. Individual members of the group would have access by right to the finance or services involved. This is an important and valuable approach to targeting in that it secures access by group members to the resources on a long-term guaranteed basis. Access is no longer determined by changing political will, by the discretion of local service providers or by changing levels of resources available to the exchequer. A rights based approach to targeting is also important as an acknowledgement of the value of the full participation in society by the group targeted and of the need to guarantee this participation.

The Minister for Finance, Brian Cowen TD, dedicated a quarter of his first budget day financial statement to disability issues in December 2004. This reflected a remarkable and unique emphasis in such a speech. He stated 'My strong view, based on my experience as Minister for Health, is that the disability programme was for many years at the end of the queue for resources. It did not benefit from the type of professional lobbying and support which the acute hospital and primary care programmes traditionally got from strong organised interests in the health services'[1] – a statement that reveals the real impact of inequalities of representation and power in Irish society. Targeted initiatives that involve transferring resources to meet the needs of groups experiencing inequality are unlikely in the absence of strong organised interests. In that budget the Minister for Finance highlighted that the Expenditure Estimates for 2005 of €2.8 billion for people with disabilities 'represented an increase of €290 million or 11% on the 2004 figure'. He announced a special disability multi-annual funding package of close to €900 million for 2006 to 2009 stating 'this package includes guaranteed additional current spending of almost €600 million. The Government has also agreed to allocate €300 million out of the revised capital envelopes to which I referred earlier to those high priority disability services.'[2] This new targeted investment is timely, welcome and necessary. However, as yet it has been impossible to gauge to what extent this new investment will be adequate to meeting the needs of people with disabilities.

The National Disability Strategy includes a valuable development of administrative systems in some Government Departments for a better inclusion of people with disabilities. These new administrative systems include the preparation of sectoral plans by six Government Departments for their services to people with disabilities. These new administrative systems are important. However, they could have been more broadly applied. Sectoral plans could usefully have been required of all Government Departments and State agencies.

New administrative systems also include a needs assessment process set out in the Disability Bill 2004. The needs assessment is to be carried out by an assessment officer of the Health

Board. It is to be confined to assessing the health and education needs of the person with disabilities and the services considered appropriate to meet these needs. A liaison officer of the health board is then to prepare a service statement on foot of the needs assessment identifying what services will actually be provided. This is a very limited approach that is proposed. It does not address the full spectrum of needs of the person with disabilities and it does not guarantee that the services considered appropriate will be made available.

The Comhairle (Amendment) Bill 2004 provides for limited access to advocacy for some people with disabilities. This is a further element to the new administrative systems envisaged in the National Disability Strategy. Access to a personal advocate is limited in that the service is only made available to a person with disabilities when the Director of Comhairle is of the opinion that not only would the person be unable to obtain a particular social service or service without the support of a personal advocate but that there are also reasonable grounds to believe that there is a risk of harm to the health, welfare or safety of the person if they are not provided with the social service or service. A broader more widely available and more diverse advocacy service would better meet the needs of all people with disabilities.

The National Disability Strategy is underpinned by the Disability Bill 2004 and the Comhairle (Amendment) Bill 2004. This legislation is the weakest element in the strategy because of its limitations. The Disability Bill 2004 is limited in that the definition of people with disabilities is narrow and will create a hierarchy among different groups of people with disabilities. It marks a significant move away from the inclusive definition used in the equality legislation. It excludes significant groups who don't come within the definition but who require access to the services covered by the legislation.

There is a failure in the Bill to ringfence resources for disability services and to afford rights to people with disabilities in terms of service entitlements. The only right is to a needs assessment and even this appears compromised by the manner in which the Bill deals with resource issues. This would appear to limit services envisaged by the Bill to a residual situation where funding is only made available after all other responsibilities are met.

The manner in which resources are dealt with in the Bill could undermine already existing protections in equality legislation. A claim cannot be made under the Equal Status Acts if it relates to something that is required by another piece of legislation. The Equal Status Acts require providers of goods and services and providers of accommodation and educational establishments not to discriminate against people with disabilities either directly or indirectly. However, indirect discrimination may be allowed if it is objectively justified by a legitimate aim and the means of achieving that aim are appropriate and necessary. The Acts require providers of goods and service and providers of accommodation and educational establishments to make reasonable accommodation for people with disabilities subject to a nominal cost exemption. These obligations may require the allocation of resources. The Disability Bill would appear to allow public sector service providers to argue as a defence to a claim for discrimination that they are obliged by the Bill in certain circumstances not to allocate resources to services to people with disabilities envisaged by the Bill unless all their other funding responsibilities have been met. The Disability Bill could thus be used as a defence to claims of direct or indirect discrimination on the disability ground or in relation to reasonable accommodation under the Equal Status Act.

The provisions in the Disability Bill on access to buildings and services would appear to fall short of the reasonable accommodation requirements under the Equal Status Acts. The provisions in the Disability Bill apply to a far smaller group of people. They are dependent on the provisions in the Bill in relation to resource allocation. Buildings must be accessible as far as practicable by 2015. The provisions in relation to services are limited to ensuring access is integrated. A far more effective approach would have been to require reasonable accommodation for public service users with disabilities subject to the exemption that applies in relation to employment where the employer is required to make reasonable accommodation of employees with disabilities unless this imposes a disproportionate burden. This would build on and enhance the equality legislation.[3]

This disability legislation reflects a marked and unfortunate reluctance to further develop a rights based approach to equality – an approach that was valuably initiated on the disability ground in the equality legislation. Targeted initiatives within a strategic framework for action on equality should be underpinned by legislative entitlements if they are to achieve their full impact. The disability legislation also reflects a reluctance to further develop and evolve current equality legislation. The provisions in relation to reasonable accommodation by public sector service providers could have been strengthened without falling foul of the Constitutional provisions in relation to private property. A statutory duty could have been placed on the public sector to have due regard to equality for people with disabilities in carrying out their functions. A statutory duty could have secured a comprehensive and sustained focus on achieving equality for people with disabilities across all of the public sector. This statutory duty could have underpinned and shaped the proposed sectoral plans. A valuable opportunity in this regard has been missed.

TARGETING FOR EMPOWERMENT AND CAPACITY BUILDING

Targeted initiatives can support equality objectives of enhancing access to new and greater levels of resources for groups experiencing inequality. They can also support equality objectives in relation to access to decision making by assisting such groups to develop organisations with a capacity to advocate on their behalf and to articulate their interests in decision making that impacts on them. Such targeted initiatives empower groups experiencing inequality by enhancing their access to decision-making processes. They support a new capacity within these groups to participate effectively in these decision-making processes.

The National Anti-Poverty Networks Programme and the Community Development Programme provide valuable examples of targeted initiatives that include an emphasis on empowerment of those currently experiencing inequality. Both programmes originated in the then Department of Social Community and Family Affairs. Their implementation and management were the responsibility of the Combat Poverty Agency – the statutory body established to advise the Government on economic and social issues pertaining to poverty. Currently both programmes are the sole responsibility of the Department of Community, Rural and Gaeltacht Affairs.

The National Anti-Poverty Networks Programme is designed to assist national representative or coordinating organisations to develop their capacity to contribute to policy development at national level and to draw policy lessons from their experiences at local and national level. It provides core funding, advice and support, and opportunities for joint policy development to the national networks. The anti-poverty focus is defined as one key characteristic of these networks as is their role in giving voice to disadvantaged and marginalised groups in local, regional and national fora.

This funding programme includes organisations representing people with disabilities, lone parents, Travellers, refugees and older women. It supports an organisational capacity at national level to articulate, advocate and negotiate the interests of these groups. It contributes to the equality objective of participation in decision-making by these groups and provides a platform from which they can pursue other equality objectives in terms of access to resources, to status and to relationships of love, care and solidarity. This targeting should be further extended to include all groups from across the nine grounds experiencing inequality and without access to the resources needed for this level of organisation. This would contribute to a coherent support for the participation of all these groups in decision-making that impacts on them and enhance the achievement of this core equality objective of political equality.

The aim of the Community Development Programme is defined as 'to enhance the capacity of disadvantaged communities to participate fully in society'. Local groups are funded so that they can:

- develop a greater capacity to influence others and articulate their point of view;
- have a role in decisions that affect them;
- contribute to a process of change in their areas;
- improve their quality of life.

This important funding programme resources nearly 190 different groups. Many of these are area based. However, around one third of them work with specific communities of interest. Groups working with women and groups working with Travellers are particularly prominent in this regard. There are also groups funded who are working with lone parents, minority ethnic communities other than Travellers, men, older people and people with disabilities. The programme could also usefully expand to secure an adequate inclusion of organisations that work with the full diversity of groups covered by the equality legislation. This would secure a presence or a greater presence for gay and lesbian groups, carer groups, minority ethnic communities, disability groups, older people's groups, men's groups and lone parents in the programme. It would allow further growth in the number of women's groups and Traveller groups in the programme. This would assist in a coherent support for the pursuit of equality objectives of representation for these different groups.

Good practice in community development within communities experiencing inequality is central to realising such equality objectives. Community development involves providing support for these communities to organise at local level, to identify their shared concerns and aspirations and to articulate these to good effect in decision-making arenas. It builds a capacity within these communities to have a real say in decisions that affect them. It supports an advocacy for the rights of these communities as a group and as individuals. Inevitably, the practice of community development can be of a variable quality and does not always live up to this good practice standard. It is important that this good practice standard continues to be promoted, encouraged and supported if community development strategies are to realise their full potential in promoting equality.

Community development with its emphasis on community organisation is critical in realising political equality objectives of access to decision-making. Effective community organisations can lobby, advocate with and negotiate with policy makers and service providers. They can thus have an influence over the allocation of and access to resources. Effective community organisations can secure a public profile for the experience and situation of their community. They can therefore shape new perceptions of the community and challenge stereotypes. This work contributes to equality in access to status and a valuing of their diversity and to building new relationships of solidarity and support with other communities.

It is important that initiatives targeted on groups experiencing inequality continue to include this focus on empowerment and capacity building if objectives of political equality are to be achieved. These initiatives require funding sources, such as the two described above, that cover the core costs of community organisations and that are committed to resourcing participation in decision-making by these organisations. The participation of these groups in decision-making involves an independent and sometimes angry voice in giving expression to experiences and situations of inequality and to demands for greater equality. It must also be an empowered voice with access to resources to ensure it gets a hearing.

Participation in decision-making poses challenges to organisations that seek to articulate the interests of those experiencing inequality. An empowered voice is also a voice with capacity. Capacity building is needed for these organisations so that they have access to necessary information and knowledge, to skills for lobby work, advocacy and negotiation, and to skills necessary to build the organisation and sustain its accountability back into the community experiencing inequality. This capacity building requires that funding organisations provide financial resources for training and personal development and for mentoring and other forms of support to these organisations and their members.

TARGETING FOR CARING EQUALITY

Caring equality is concerned with access to relationships of love, care and solidarity. Public policy and institutional practices can shape access to relationships of care. Targeted initiatives within work life balance arrangements in the workplace, for example, can assist parents and carers to reconcile working and caring responsibilities. Targeted initiatives within policy making can also facilitate people in playing caring roles.

The Parental Leave Bill 2004, which was brought forward by the Department of Justice, Equality and Law Reform, provides an example, if somewhat limited, of a targeted initiative concerned with relationships of care and caring equality objectives. The original Parental Leave Act 1998 sought to give effect to an EU Directive on parental leave (96/34/EC). It provided for an entitlement for men and women to avail of unpaid leave from employment to care for their young children. It also provided for limited paid leave (force majeure leave) to enable employees to deal with family emergencies resulting from injury or illness of a family member.

The uptake of this unpaid leave has been low. Nearly 7% of the workforce was estimated to be eligible for this leave in the April 2002 *Report of the Working Group on the Review of Parental Leave Act.*[4] It was estimated that 20% of those eligible took up their entitlement. Eighty-four per cent of parental leave taken was taken by women. No provision is made for paternity leave. The unpaid leave must be taken before the child reaches 5 years of age and is limited to fourteen weeks for each parent for each child.

The parental leave legislation was a limited targeted initiative to support equality in the caring arena. The absence of paid parental leave, the lack of paternity leave and the limited leave period available place Ireland behind many of its EU counterparts in this provision. A comparative study in four European countries, including Ireland, of work-life balance issues identified that Danish parents were found to exhibit the highest levels of well being. This was linked to:

• the relatively even distribution of working hours between the sexes (backed up by a more equal distribution of household chores between mothers and fathers);
• a high level of relatively cheap public day-care provision widely acknowledged and appreciated;
• a generous provision of paid maternity and parental leave;
• a workplace culture exhibiting a relatively relaxed and supportive attitude towards the problem of reconciling work and family life.[5]

The current situation in relation to parental leave suggests that these factors are weak in the Irish context. The take up of parental leave reflects an imbalance in the sharing of caring between women and men. The leave entitlement is unpaid and far from generous in the length of time afforded, of fourteen weeks for each parent. The low level of take up can in part be attributed to a workplace culture not attuned to the needs of people with caring responsibilities. The Parental Leave Bill 2004 provided an opportunity for a new and more effective targeting for caring equality.

The Bill raised the maximum age of the eligible child to 8 years (16 years in the case of a child with disabilities). It extended parental leave entitlement to those acting *in loco parentis* (an important development for foster parents and same sex partners). It allowed the leave to be taken in separate blocks. However, it did not extend the leave that could be taken. It did not introduce payment for this leave period. It did not introduce paternity leave. The new legislation, therefore, offers little to further enhance parental well being and the care afforded to children.

TARGETING TO MEET NEEDS SPECIFIC TO A GROUP

Targeted initiatives described in previous sections seek to play important roles in advancing equality in access to resources (National Disability Strategy), to decision-making (National Anti-Poverty Networks Programme and Community Development Programme) and to relationships of care (Parental Leave legislation). These roles are important in addressing inequalities based on a past legacy of discrimination and exclusion. Targeted initiatives will also be required in a future context of greater equality, even after this legacy has been effectively addressed. Even in this context of greater equality such initiatives will continue to contribute to meeting needs that are specific to a group because of its particular identity, experience or situation.

The Traveller accommodation programme provides an example of a targeted initiative that seeks to meet needs specific to a particular group. Travellers have specific accommodation needs due to their cultural traditions of nomadism.[6] The Task Force on the Traveller Community defined Traveller nomadism as taking a range of forms. 'This includes those who are constantly on the move, those who move out from a fixed base for a part of any year, and those who are sedentary for many years and then move on.'[7] It highlighted how Traveller nomadism contributes to the social organisation of the community, the important economic role it plays and the psychological importance it holds for Travellers. Traveller nomadism creates a context of needs and aspirations that are specific to the Traveller community. This has been responded to by local authorities and national Government with Traveller accommodation provision that includes a mix of standard houses, group housing schemes for Travellers, Traveller halting sites and temporary sites. The Task Force highlighted the need to include in this list a network of transient sites to facilitate Traveller nomadism and to phase out the use of temporary sites.

Since the report of the Task Force on the Travelling Community there has been significant developments in relation to targeted initiatives for Traveller accommodation. These have principally been at the level of legislation and institutional development. The Housing (Traveller Accommodation) Act 1998 was the first piece of legislation specifically dedicated to addressing the situation of Travellers. It requires local authorities to assess the need for Traveller halting sites and to prepare and implement a five year Traveller accommodation programme.

In terms of institutional development the legislation established the National Traveller Accommodation Consultative Committee which advises the Minister for the Environment and Local Government in relation to any general matter in relation to Traveller accommodation issues. This includes representatives from the three national Traveller organisations (Irish Traveller Movement, National Traveller Women's Forum and Pavee Point). Local Authorities are required under the legislation to set up Traveller accommodation consultative committees. These involve Councillors, local authority officials and local Traveller organisations. The role of these committees is to advise on the preparation of local Traveller accommodation programmes.

This reflects an impressive range of developments. However,

where this targeted initiative has failed is in relation to implementation. As noted in Chapter One, in 2003 there was a total of 1,738 Traveller families with no permanent accommodation. This accounted for 30% of all Traveller families. The report of the Task Force on the Travelling Community in 1995 had estimated a need for 3,100 units of accommodation for Traveller families and recommended that these be provided by 2000. Three years after the target date set, less than half of these units had been provided according to the annual count figures prepared by the Department of Environment and Local Government in 2003.

Budgets, legislation, policies and programmes reflect a broad range of targeted initiatives seeking to promote equality for particular groups of people These include the Equality for Women measure under the National Development Plan, the carers leave legislation and carer allowances, income support for lone parents, health services targeting older people and people with disabilities, legislation in relation to the education of people with disabilities, Traveller specific training programmes, educational resources to support the inclusion of minority ethnic pupils in schools and health projects targeting gay and lesbian people. This is a dimension of the strategic framework for action on equality that is well developed. However, the examples given reflect the need to further develop the design, implementation and ambition of these targeted initiatives.

POTENTIAL PITFALLS IN TARGETING

Targeting is an important dimension within the strategic framework for action on equality. However, there are pitfalls that have been associated with some targeted initiatives. These can be illustrated by examining a number of targeted initiatives. Traveller education has involved significant targeted initiatives. The pitfalls associated with this targeted provision relate to the quality of the objectives established for the initiatives, the experience of segregation that resulted from special provision and the limited impact of the targeted initiatives. Service provision to people with disabilities has involved significant targeted initiatives. The pitfalls associated with this targeted provision relates to standards and the quality of service provided. Finally, carers and their access to community care services has also involved significant targeted initiatives. The pitfalls associated with this targeted provision relates to levels of investment and the capacity of the provisions to meet the demand for it.

Traveller Education

The Report of the Commission on Itinerancy was published in August 1963. The Commission identified its central objective in the following terms: 'It is not considered that there is any alternative to a positive drive for housing itinerants if a permanent solution of the problem of itinerancy, based on absorption and integration, is to be achieved'.[8] This central objective was one of assimilation. This objective placed no value on, and accorded no status to, Traveller culture and identity. It was an objective based on imposing the norms and values of the dominant settled cultural group on the minority nomadic cultural group. Such an objective could not contribute to equality given that it runs counter to objectives of cultural equality and of political equality.

The Commission identified the provision of education as playing a key role in achieving this central objective of assimilation. The report stated that providing a basic education to Traveller children was urgent 'both as a means of providing opportunities for a better way of life and of promoting their absorption into the settled community'.[9]

Only 160 Traveller children were on the school rolls in November 1960 according to the Commission. This contrasted with census figures from December 1960 which showed 1,642 Traveller children between the ages of 6 and 14 years. The Commission recommended a strategy of targeting specific education provision at the Traveller community other than for children aged 7 or under who should commence school in the ordinary way.

A stimulus for new targeted initiatives to provide education for Travellers was provided by the Commission. However, these were based on objectives of assimilation. This assimilationist approach sought to absorb the Traveller community into the culture of the majority settled community. Over twenty years later, with limited progress made in improving the educational status of Travellers, the Task Force on the Travelling community highlighted that such an approach has been 'criticised for being patronising and dismissive of other cultures and for being racist'.[10]

The Report of the Travelling People Review Body in February 1983 noted this limited progress in that school attendance figures represented only about half the Traveller children of school going age. It further noted that few Traveller children remained in school after the age of 12 years and that 'even those children who attend school regularly seldom obtain maximum educational benefit without additional help'.[11] The Report outlined the development of 30 pre-school classes for Traveller children, the establishment of two special schools for Travellers in Dublin and Wicklow and more than 70 special classes for Travellers in schools.

A targeting approach was endorsed by the Review Body. It highlighted the need to increase Traveller pre-school classes to cater for all Traveller children of this age: 'the need for additional special schools must be considered for any areas where large numbers of families are congregated under adverse living conditions' and 'that special classes have an important contribution to make to the education of traveller children' but that such provision should be seen as an interim measure. It recommended a further extension of this targeting with 'the provision as a matter of extreme urgency, of special educational and vocational facilities for Traveller children between the ages of 12 and 15 years' and 'the extension of present training centre facilities to provide education and training opportunities for at least 700 young travellers'.[12]

The Review Body reflected some continuity with the analysis of the Commission suggesting an objective for education for Travellers as 'to give them freedom to make a real choice about their future way of life'. The Review Body had started with a promising and valuable definition of Travellers:

> They are an identifiable group of people, identified both by themselves and by other members of the community

(referred to for convenience as the "settled community") as people with their own distinctive lifestyle, traditionally of a nomadic nature but not now habitual wanderers. They have needs, wants and values which are different in some ways from those of the settled community.[13]

This definition was somewhat undermined when an underlying thinking emerged in the recommendation that 'newly wed couples who have to occupy caravans following their marriage should be considered extra sympathetically for housing to lessen the risks of regression to a travelling way of life'.[14] Objectives of absorption and assimilation that influenced the Commission clearly held some sway within the Review Body.

Evidence of limited impact from targeted provision being made was provided by the Review Body. However, they failed to move away from the flawed objective of assimilation that informed this targeted provision. They promoted an approach of integration which acknowledges difference and the need for specific economic and social supports for minorities such as Travellers. However, this integration approach involves an understanding of difference that is based on people choosing to be different or to integrate. The approach seeks to influence that supposed choice in a manner that realises an integration of the minority group within the dominant culture so that ultimately a homogenous society is created. There is some limited commitment to cultural equality in this approach. However, this is based on a flawed assumption that people can make choices as to their identity and the culture they belong to. The integration approach also involves some limited commitment to political equality. However, this is based on affording limited choice – the choice of integration is resourced, the alternative is not.

The Report of the Task Force on the Travelling Community in 1995 marked a transformation in analysis and practice that had begun to take place in the period since the Review Body. The starting point for the Task Force was 'that the distinct culture and identity of the Traveller community be recognised and taken into account'.[15] The Task Force promoted a mainstreaming approach. Economic and social supports needed to be targeted at Travellers. However, at the same time mainstream institutions including schools needed to adapt to take account of cultural diversity.

The Task Force highlighted growth in pre-school provision with fifty-six pre-schools for Traveller children. It noted that 4,200 Traveller children attended primary school out of approximately 5,000 Traveller children. This provision included four special schools for Travellers and 200 special classes for Travellers. However, it also highlighted limited progress in stating that 'the poor performance of many Traveller children in primary school deeply concerns many Travellers and their teachers'. It noted a report 'that only approximately 100 Traveller children aged 12 to 15 years were attending mainstream second-level schools out of the estimated 2,000 children eligible to do so'.[16]

The danger of segregation that can accompany targeted provision was raised by the Task Force. It put forward that 'the principle of integration should be applied save in exceptional circumstances' as a fundamental principle to be applied in education provision. It reacted with alarm to some of the recommendations of a 1992 Report of the Department of Education Working Group on Post Primary Education for Traveller Children stating that some of the recommendations made 'might result in a segregationist policy towards Travellers. Travellers in general abhor the experience and the negative results of segregationist policies in former and in some current primary school provision for Travellers. Care must be taken not to repeat these at second level.'[17]

Service provision to people with disabilities

Another pitfall that can be associated with targeting becomes evident when the experience of people with disabilities is considered. There are potential pitfalls in relation to standards and quality in targeted initiatives. There is a risk of low standards where services are targeted on a group that is marginalised, excluded and disempowered. The Report of the Commission on the Status of People with Disabilities reflects the importance of services that target the needs of people with disabilities. It emphasises the right of people with disabilities 'to quality services which meet their needs at all stages of life and they must not be dependent on charity or voluntary effort'.[18]

The Commission recommended that 'all services to people with disabilities should have quality assurance systems in place. All service providing organisations should also be asked to produce clear quality standards for the services they offer and to put in place performance monitoring systems, including feedback from people with disabilities. Each organisation should also be required to offer disability awareness training to all staff.'[19]

Quin and Redmond raise the issue of standards in service provision in their overview of social policy for people with disability. They highlight: 'People with disabilities living in residential care are another group whose rights may be infringed. Basic, everyday decisions about when and what to eat, when to get up and go to bed, have a bath or shower, deciding where and when to go out may be determined by staff rostering rather than the wishes of adult residents.'[20] They suggest that 'the development of services provided by such voluntary bodies has been limited by unreliable and often inadequate state funding' and that 'the widespread use of voluntary organisations to provide services has also resulted in an unequal or variable distribution of services geographically.' They also highlight 'the growing public disquiet with conditions of care for those with intellectual disability' since the 1970s – a disquiet that continues to the present day.

In 2004 the National Disability Authority and the Department of Health and Children published National Standards for Disability Services. These aim to ensure:

(a) that the safety, dignity, independence and well being of service users are protected and promoted;

(b) that person-centred service provision is established and nurtured in all services; and

(c) that all services are provided to an agreed level of quality and performance and that the level of quality is consistent on a national basis.[21]

The standards are designed to apply 'to all statutory and non-statutory agencies that provide health related disability services for children and adults with autism, intellectual, physical and/or sensory disability funded by the Department of Health and Children'.[22] The standards are to operate as a quality framework with minimum criteria to be met for the service to be recognised as an approved service. Meeting further criteria will be acknowledged by 'approved with quality' and 'approved with excellence' recognition. The assessment is to be carried out by an external assessment body, with non compliance reported to the Department of Health and Children and access to an independent appeals committee if necessary.

The standards focus on person centred services, good governance within organisations, dignity at work for employees, effective information and communication and safe environments. These standards are not ambitious. They reflect a basic foundation for quality. Despite this, there are anecdotal reports of dissatisfaction among service providers. This must be a cause for concern if such basic standards are found to stretch the current approach by service providers. It must also be a cause for concern that the assessment process has yet to be implemented beyond an initial pilot scheme.

Carers' access to services

A final potential pitfall in relation to targeting involves the need to ensure an adequacy of investment in such targeting. Inadequate investment in targeting results in underdeveloped and unevenly spread services. This can lead to further inequalities. The experience of carers in relation to the need for community care services highlights this issue.

Research has been carried out on carers who seek to combine paid employment and caring responsibilities.[23] This includes a particular focus on community care services to people with disabilities and to older people and the contribution this targeted provision makes to equality for carers at work and equality between carers in different areas and caring situations.

This research found that 'all community health and social services, including those potentially useful to working carers, are under-developed, in short supply and often unequally available across health boards and community care areas. Also, those services that are available are not provided to a time schedule that takes account of the needs of working carers.'

The research highlighted that these services 'are less likely to be provided if there are family members who can provide care and the fact that such potential carers may be working or may desire to be working may not necessarily be taken into consideration'. The 'wide variation across health boards and areas within health boards in terms of what services are available and in the accessibility of the services that are available' can generate significant inequalities between carers with similar needs in terms of caring responsibilities or similar aspiration in terms of participation in other areas of life including paid employment.

MAINSTREAMING

In a speech to an Equality Authority conference on Equality Mainstreaming, President Mary McAleese made the point:

> Build inclusion and equality in from the beginning and get an outcome that is not skewed. Fail to do so and skewed outcomes become millstones around our necks.[24]

Mainstreaming ensures equality is a factor in decision-making about key policies, programmes and practices. It involves gathering data, knowledge and information on groups experiencing inequality and applying these in decision-making. This contributes to effective decision-making by ensuring an evidence basis for the decisions made and counters the potential for false assumptions or negative stereotypes of groups within the nine grounds to shape decision-making. Mainstreaming involves stimulating an awareness of equality among decision makers when policies, programmes and practices are being designed and challenges any indifference relating to equality by decision makers. It involves the participation in the decision-making process of organisations representing groups experiencing inequality. This participation introduces a further democracy into decision-making. Mainstreaming is integral to planning and policy making processes already in place within an organisation. This limits any additional administrative burden on decision makers who pursue a mainstreaming approach. Mainstreaming has a capacity to achieve institutional change through new attitudes among decision makers and through new practices being developed by decision makers within the organisation. It has the potential to prevent discrimination and new inequalities emerging as a result of new policies, programmes and practices while also achieving a coherence between general policies, programmes and practices and targeted initiatives promoting equality.

Mainstreaming was developed as a concept and a practice within the European Commission. The European Commission focused on gender equality and gender mainstreaming. It influenced practice by the Member States as gender main-streaming was introduced as a requirement in the use of EU Structural Funds. A wider equality mainstreaming that encompasses all nine grounds covered by the equality legislation has been developed in Ireland. Equality mainstreaming has been developed as a concept and promoted as a practice in particular by the social partners. It has been designed and piloted by the Equality Authority in the preparation of the strategy plans of the City and County Development Boards, in the integrated poverty and equality proofing of two policy initiatives and in a scheme of employment equality reviews within a range of organisations. These various initiatives at EU level and in the Irish context are now explored.

EU and Gender Mainstreaming

In 1996 the European Commission published a Communica-tion setting out the European Union's objective to mainstream measures for equality between women and men into all European Union policies. It highlighted that this process would produce a cultural transformation of attitudes and collective practices. It defined gender mainstreaming as:

Not restricting efforts to promote equality to the implementation of specific measures to help women, but mobilising all general policies and measures specifically for the purpose of achieving equality by actively and openly taking into account at the planning stage their possible effects on the respective situations of men and women.[25]

Gender mainstreaming is thus part of a dual strategy of specific measures targeting women and of gender mainstreaming within all policies and measures. Gender mainstreaming was further developed as an approach by the Treaty of Amsterdam in 1997. Article 2EC establishes gender equality as an explicit objective of the Community and Article 3EC imposes an obligation on the Community to eliminate inequalities and to promote equality between men and women in all its activities.

Gender Mainstreaming and the Structural Funds

The Structural Funds is the general title given to European Union funding which seeks to bring about cohesion between EU Member States. The principal Structural Funds are the European Regional Development Fund, directed at areas such as transport, industry, tourism and infrastructure, and the European Social Fund which is directed at areas such as education, training and human resources development. New regulations were introduced to govern the use of the Structural Funds in the Member States for the period 2000 to 2006. These included a requirement that the operations of the Funds were to be consistent with other Community policies and operations, in particular equality between men and women (EC 1260/99 Article 2). This means that Structural Fund policies and programmes have to be gender mainstreamed.

Ireland has incorporated EU Structural Fund resources and national exchequer resources to fund the National Development Plan 2000 to 2006. The Plan provides funding of nearly €51 billion over the seven year period 2000 to 2006. The Government committed to gender mainstreaming in all but six of the 177 measures and sub measures funded under the Plan. These cover transport, health and accommodation, infrastructure, education and training, industrial development and regional development and social inclusion.

Two units were established to monitor and advise on gender mainstreaming National Development Plan policies and programmes. One unit is in the Department of Education and Science with a remit in relation to the policies and programmes of that Department covered by the Plan. The second unit is in the Department of Justice, Equality and Law Reform with a remit to monitor and support gender mainstreaming across all National Development Plan policies and programmes. An Equal Opportunities and Social Inclusion Coordinating Committee is also in place to report on these issues to the main committee responsible for monitoring the implementation of the overall National Development Plan.

This commitment and the infrastructure put in place to support it is impressive in that it seeks to apply gender mainstreaming not only to EU Structural Funds in the National Development Plan but also to exchequer funds, and in that the process of gender mainstreaming is both supported and monitored. The development of gender mainstreaming is important in terms of an emerging capacity for gender mainstreaming to take its place within the strategic framework for action on equality. However, progress has been uneven. McGauren and Crowley (Author) note:

> In relation to the requirement that equal opportunities be incorporated into project selection criteria, only 37% of 177 measures and sub measures in the NDP include this criterion and 47% do not include it at all. In terms of gender disaggregated indicators, 44% of measures and sub measures do commit to collecting these indicators and 19% commit to developing gender disaggregated data, but 24% have no such commitment. And on the monitoring committees, although the recommended representation of women is 40%, in 2002 on three of the six main monitoring committees women comprised less than one quarter of the representatives.[26]

Gender mainstreaming is breaking new ground in terms of equality strategies in an Irish context. The experience of gender mainstreaming provides valuable learning on how best to implement a wider equality mainstreaming. The gender mainstreaming infrastructure developed provides an important foundation for the further development of a wider equality mainstreaming. The social partners have taken on to promote this further development of mainstreaming in a broader range of policy areas and with a broader focus across the nine grounds covered by the equality legislation.

SOCIAL PARTNERS AND EQUALITY MAINSTREAMING

The social partners have made a valuable contribution in bringing forward a commitment to this wider equality main-streaming under the term 'Equality Proofing' and in seeking progress on such an approach within national policy making and programme development. The term equality proofing is used with the same meaning as equality mainstreaming.

As early as 1996 the National Economic and Social Forum (NESF) produced a report entitled 'Equality Proofing Issues'.[27] This identified equality proofing as 'a mechanism, process or technical method to implement equality objectives built into a variety of social and economic policies'. It recommended that equality proofing should be seen as an essential principle to be implemented by all Government Departments and State Agencies.

This report has influenced three subsequent national agreements. These national agreements include commitments that reflect a growing understanding of equality proofing (equality mainstreaming) and a growing practice of this approach within policy making. Partnership 2000 for Inclusion, Employment and Competitiveness stated that:

> In the context of the NAPS (National Anti-Poverty Strategy), this will be complemented by the strengthening of administrative procedures for equality proofing, having regard to the recommendations of the NESF.[28]

The Programme for Prosperity and Fairness national agreement stated that

> The Partnership 2000 report on Equality Proofing will inform the development of equality proofing. An initial learning phase of proofing will be commenced during 2000 and its core elements will reflect recommendations contained in the Report.[29]

The Sustaining Progress national agreement stated that:

> Proofing of policies and services in the public sector to

avoid unanticipated negative impact on any of the groups protected under the equality legislation to ensure policy coherence and best use of resources will build on the experience of gender proofing under the NDP, the Working Group on Equality Proofing and experience of poverty proofing.[30]

Throughout this period a working group of the social partners has sought to stimulate and support the implementation of these commitments. This is convened by the Department of Justice, Equality and Law Reform. It includes the four pillars to social partnership, the Office of Social Inclusion, the Combat Poverty Agency, the Gender Mainstreaming Unit, the Equality Commission for Northern Ireland and the Equality Authority.

The working group produced a report in January 2000. In this it 'articulated a vision of a single integrated equality proofing process'.[31] An integrated approach to mainstreaming would incorporate gender mainstreaming developed within the context of the National Development Plan, poverty proofing as established under the National Anti-Poverty Strategy and equality proofing covering the nine grounds in the equality legislation. In its longer term vision the working group identified a value in generating ideas on how best to proceed in relation to putting in place a firm legal basis for equality proofing. It identified a value in such a legal basis in ensuring:

- certainty as to the requirements of a proofing process;
- consistency in the implementation of proofing procedures;
- the availability of review and enforcement mechanisms;
- a firm basis for public participation and consultation;
- a permanent and stable basis for proofing procedures;
- an open transparent and accountable proofing process.[32]

The report recommended a learning phase for equality proofing. This learning phase would build a knowledge basis around the practical implementation of equality proofing across nine different grounds on a par with the knowledge base already developed in relation to gender mainstreaming and poverty proofing. Three equality proofing initiatives have been implemented by the Equality Authority as part of this learning phase which generated particular learning in terms of building an equality mainstreaming approach into policy development and programme design. These initiatives covered work on equality proofing of the Strategy Plans of the City and County Development Boards, a pilot approach in two policy areas to integrated proofing that encompassed a focus on equality and poverty, and a programme of employment equality reviews.

City and County Development Boards and Equality Proofing

City and County Development Boards are established within each local authority. They include key organisations at local authority level and seek to stimulate a coordinated and coherent approach to development at this level. They were required by the Department of Environment and Local Government to develop and implement ten year strategy plans. The work on equality mainstreaming developed by the Equality Authority with the City and County Development Boards included designing a template to provide guidance on equality proofing their strategy plans and developing a template to support an equality impact assessment on any new measures to be implemented as part of the strategy plans. These templates included all nine grounds covered by the equality legislation.

These templates identify diversity as a key focus in assessing the impact of policies or programmes on equality. Diversity is understood in terms of:

- identity – the values and norms held by a particular group;
- experience – the relationships between the group members and service providers and the wider society;
- situation – the status of the group in terms of resources, housing, labour market, education etc.[33]

Both templates are based on a test of the capacity of the policy or programme in its design and delivery to take account of and accommodate the diversity of relevant groups experiencing inequality.

The methodology developed to carry out an equality impact assessment provides key learning from this initiative.[34] Seven key steps are identified as central to this equality mainstreaming process. The first step relates to selecting which policies or programmes should be a focus for an equality impact assessment. The second step relates to selecting which groups from across the nine grounds should be included in the assessment. It is necessary to be strategic in the selection of policies or programmes so that those chosen for an equality impact assessment are those with significant potential to progress equality objectives. The policy or programme should be selected for its scale in terms of expenditure and national relevance and for its scope in terms of the change it will bring about and for whom this change would be relevant. It is necessary to be inclusive in the selection of groups for inclusion in the equality impact assessment so as to ensure the policy or programme has a capacity to accommodate and benefit all groups experiencing inequality that are relevant to the focus of the policy or programme. The groups should be identified for the extent to which their diversity could have practical implications for the policy or programme.

The third step involves those designing the policy or programme in gathering data on the selected groups. The data gathered will provide relevant information on the situation, the experience and the identity of the particular groups. It will include statistical data and more qualitative information and data. The data gathered should assist those designing the policy or programme to identify the key issues for the groups in relation to the matters to be addressed by the policy or programme. The fourth step involves those designing the policy or programme in assessing its impact on the selected groups. They analyse the data gathered to assess whether the policy or programme as designed and delivered will accommodate, or take account of, the practical implications of the diversity of the selected groups and what changes might be necessary to ensure this diversity is adequately accommodated.

The fifth step involves the participation of organisations that can represent and articulate the interests of those groups identified as part of the impact assessment. This participation will allow a dialogue between these organisations and those designing the policy or programme to explore the quality of the data gathered and of the impact assessment made. Further changes to the policy or programme could be identified as necessary on foot of this dialogue. The sixth step involves those designing the policy or programme in making a final decision on this design. The policy or programme should then be monitored for its impact on the selected groups during its implementation. Monitoring is the seventh and final step and will require collecting and analysing data on the impact of the policy or programme.

Integrated Equality and Poverty Proofing

Integrated equality and poverty proofing draws from the experience of gender mainstreaming within the National Development Plan, poverty proofing under the National Anti-Poverty Strategy and equality proofing initiatives that encompass the nine grounds covered by the equality legislation. Administrative simplicity in mainstreaming in policy making can be achieved with a single integrated proofing process encompassing both poverty and equality. A focus on the intersection between the experiences of poverty and of inequality and between the different groups selected as part of the proofing process can be developed within an integrated proofing process. The multiple disadvantages and discriminations that can occur when factors such as gender, low income or rural disadvantage are combined can be highlighted in an integrated proofing process. There is, however, the danger that individual poverty or equality dimensions could be compromised or rendered invisible in a mainstreaming process that seeks to encompass such a broad range of groups.

The focus on diversity developed within equality proofing is retained within integrated poverty and equality proofing. This is explored alongside a focus on the barriers that can exclude people experiencing poverty. The template developed for the initiative[35] identifies these barriers as:

- access – which refers to geographic or physical access;
- information – encompassing the availability and accessibility of information and the communication strategies of organisations;
- disposition – encompassing the cultural attitudes and views of service providers or policy makers or of members of the groups identified;
- finance – encompassing the costs of participation whether these are direct costs or opportunity costs where other

economic opportunities are foregone to secure inclusion in an activity or service provided;

- institutions – encompassing the issues that arise where organisations have weakly developed or articulated policies, practices or procedures in relation to equality and social inclusion.

Data is gathered by those carrying out the integrated proofing process, in relation to the diversity of and the barriers faced by the groups included in the proofing process. The process of integrated proofing involves those designing policies or programmes in testing the policy or programme for its capacity to take account of the practical implications of this diversity and to address the particular barriers the groups can experience. The groups included in integrated proofing cover gender, marital status, family status, children, young people, older people, disability, religion, sexual orientation, race (including migrants), Travellers, people experiencing urban/ rural disadvantage and people on low income. The integrated proofing process follows the same seven steps developed for equality impact assessments.

During 2004 this integrated proofing was tested in two policy areas. The Equality Authority worked with the Department of Justice, Equality and Law Reform to test out this approach in finalising the National Action Plan Against Racism – a broad strategic policy document which outlines an anti-racism strategy for Ireland to be implemented by a broad range of Government Departments and State agencies. The Equality Authority worked with the Department of Social and Family Affairs to test out this approach in finalising the Back to Education Allowance Expenditure Review.

The experience of this integrated proofing initiative demonstrated that there are a range of goals that can be achieved through mainstreaming. These goals include achieving change in institutional practice, change in institutional culture and change in the experience and situation of groups experiencing inequality and poverty. Change in institutional practice was evident in the participation of non-governmental organisations in a dialogue with policy makers about final design decisions in relation to policies or programmes. This dialogue ensured that equality and poverty were considered by policy makers as factors in these final design decisions. Change in institutional culture was evident in a new awareness of equality and poverty issues among policy makers. Some policy makers involved in the initiative identified a new or deeper awareness of equality and poverty issues as one valuable impact of the initiative. Ultimately the impact of integrated proofing must be seen in change in the experience and situation of the groups experiencing poverty and inequality. The achievement of this goal will need to be assessed over time as the policy or programme is implemented.

Fears about lack of confidence in, and limited capacity for, mainstreaming were identified as barriers by all participants – non-governmental organisations and policy makers alike. Non-governmental organisations have limited resources. They expressed fears that the exercise would be irrelevant to their priorities and would not be worth putting resources into and that their contribution would not have any impact. It was difficult for the non-governmental organisations to make a contribution that was different to the consultation process about a policy or programme at an early stage in its development and that involved a more technical equality and poverty proofing of the policy or programme near final draft stage. Policy makers were apprehensive and expressed fears that the proofing process would reopen issues already decided on after consultation. They expressed fears that the dialogue with the non-governmental organisations would be critical without being constructive. As with the non-governmental organisations this was a new process for policy makers and it was difficult for policy makers to define a role for themselves within the proofing process.

It is noteworthy that the engagement of policy makers and non governmental organisations in the integrated proofing initiative quickly dispelled these fears. The constructive nature of the dialogue that developed between policy makers and non-governmental organisations built a confidence among those involved in initiatives of this kind. It is clear, however, that it will be necessary to provide ongoing external support to those involved in integrated proofing to build the knowledge, experience and skills necessary for its effective implementation.

Employment Equality Reviews

A third area of work that has been supported by the social partners and implemented by the Equality Authority is a scheme of supported and voluntary employment equality reviews and action plans within public and private sector organisations. This is an area of work that supports equality mainstreaming within the employment policies, procedures and practices of organisations. It has a particular value in bringing equality mainstreaming processes into the private sector. Prior to this, equality mainstreaming was explored only as an issue for the public sector. However, equality mainstreaming in private sector employment and service provision also has a contribution to make to a more equal society.

The employment equality reviews form part of a voluntary scheme developed by the Equality Authority. The scheme is supported by a range of funding sources. The scheme supports companies to conduct an employment equality review and prepare an equality action plan by making an independent auditor available to them alongside a template designed to guide the review and action plan. The reviews will provide valuable learning on integrating an equality focus into policies, procedures and practices at the level of the enterprise.

The independent auditor implementing the review assesses the presence, participation and situation of employees from across the nine grounds within the enterprise. Workplace policies, procedures and practices are examined by the auditor for their impact on equality. The auditor explores areas such as recruitment, promotion, working conditions and staff development. The auditor also explores existing equality strategies within the enterprise. Finally, the auditor examines perceptions within the workplace – employee perceptions of equality issues and of how effectively they see workplace policies, procedures and practices contributing to equality. A range of quantitative and qualitative methodologies are used in gathering this evidence – analysis of available data, surveys, focus groups and individual interviews.

The evidence gathered during the review provides the basis for the auditor to prepare an equality action plan for the enterprise. This plan sets out the steps to be taken to address inequalities that are identified and to mainstream an equality focus within business decision-making. The effective implementation of the plan should enhance equality outcomes for employees and potential employees from across the nine grounds and should support a workplace culture that is hostile to discrimination and harassment and supportive of diversity and equality.

FUTURE PERSPECTIVES

Mainstreaming is at an early stage of development and needs to be further evolved. Targeted initiatives are more developed and widespread than mainstreaming. Targeted initiatives need to be designed and implemented with care so that potential pitfalls of segregation, low standards and poor impact are avoided.

Future perspectives on these dimensions to the strategic framework are set out below. These focus on sustaining and developing equality mainstreaming, on maintaining a dual strategy of mainstreaming and targeting, on addressing data deficits, on developing the institutional infrastructure to implement equality mainstreaming and on supporting effective policy implementation.

Sustaining and Developing Equality Mainstreaming

The sustainability of mainstreaming came under a spotlight in a recent Opinion prepared by the Advisory Committee on Equal Opportunities between Women and Men. This Opinion criticised those responsible for the ongoing development of the EU employment strategy for the failure to mainstream a gender equality focus within a new policy document on the strategy. The Advisory Committee advises the European Commission on gender equality issues and is made up of representatives that include Member States, specialised gender equality bodies and the EU-level social partner organisations. It published an Opinion in June 2004 on the Communication from the Commission Strengthening the Implementation of the European Employment Strategy.[36]

The European Employment Strategy was agreed at the

Luxembourg jobs summit of November 1997. Guidelines were drawn up by the EU for the development of policies and programmes to promote employment, with Member States required to put in place national action plans for employment to give effect to these guidelines. The Advisory Committee had previously commented on the positive approach to gender mainstreaming within the EU Employment Strategy and the important progress made on gender equality under this strategy. In their June 2004 Opinion they highlighted that this progress is evident in 'the increasing employment rate for women, the ongoing evolution of gender mainstreaming in practice, and the introduction of a broad range of policies supporting gender equality at member state level'. The Opinion noted, however, that 'gender based discrimination in the workplace and gender inequality in the labour market has demonstrated an extraordinary persistence and resistance to change. There is urgency to further deepen and develop our response to these phenomena.'[37]

In this context it must be of concern to note the response of the Advisory Committee to the 2004 Communication from the Commission on Strengthening the Implementation of the European Employment Strategy.[38] The Opinion highlighted that 'The Advisory Committee wishes to express its concern at the virtual absence of a gender perspective in the Communication from the Commission' and went on to recommend that 'the Commission propose to the Employment Committee to renew a focus on gender mainstreaming and targeting of gender inequalities in the labour market'.[39]

This failure to incorporate a gender perspective in the Communication raises issues about the sustainability of the mainstreaming approach into the long term. This failure occurred in a policy area that had demonstrated significant commitment in the past to gender mainstreaming. As equality mainstreaming is developed in an Irish context it will be important to ensure that the systems created for this purpose can sustain this approach into the long term.

The further development of equality mainstreaming in the Irish context will need to involve integrated approaches to mainstreaming. Separate strands to mainstreaming that focus on gender, on poverty and on the nine grounds covered by the equality legislation will involve a significant administrative burden on decision makers in the absence of increased resources for mainstreaming. This administrative burden will present an insurmountable barrier to the widespread implementation of mainstreaming. Integrated approaches that adequately reflect equality and poverty priorities and secure a parity of focus on each of the selected groups provide the necessary administrative simplicity. This administrative simplicity is necessary so that integrated equality and poverty mainstreaming can be implemented by decision makers. However, at the same time mainstreaming must be carried out to a standard that is adequate to achieving practical improvements in the experience and situation of those experiencing inequality and poverty. There can be a tension between these two goals. As integrated equality and poverty mainstreaming develops, this tension should be addressed by supporting the capacity of decision makers to implement this approach, by providing adequate resources to effectively implement this approach and by monitoring its impact on poverty and inequality.

Maintaining a Dual Strategy

A dual strategy of targeting and mainstreaming is necessary. Targeted initiatives are needed to address legacies of past discrimination, to meet needs specific to groups and to secure an access for specific groups to mainstream provision. Equality mainstreaming is needed to ensure new or further inequalities and discriminations do not emerge. Targeting without mainstreaming runs the risk of low standards and segregation. Mainstreaming without targeting runs the risk of sustaining an unequal status quo due to a failure to address the legacies of past discrimination and exclusion. The failure to maintain this dual strategy is evident in the recent cross-departmental strategic framework proposed by the Office of the First Minister and Deputy First Minister to promote gender equality in Northern Ireland. The consultation document for the framework states that:

> The main emphasis in the strategy is on what can be done through policy and practice to tackle gender inequalities

using more effective gender mainstreaming. (40)

The principles established for this gender equality framework refer to 'a positive and proactive approach to identifying, understanding and responding to the needs and choices of women and men', 'avoiding the influence of stereotypes', 'promoting a partnership approach' and 'recognising multiple identities of women and men'. These principles are valuable and will usefully underpin gender mainstreaming. However, the absence of any reference to positive action or targeted initiatives raises concerns that the consultation document has failed to embrace the need for a dual strategy of targeting and mainstreaming.

Addressing Data Deficits

Effective equality mainstreaming requires that data deficits in relation to the identity, experience and situation of groups that experience inequality are addressed. Data deficits are evident in the baseline data available in relation to these groups. This is beginning to be addressed with new Census questions on carers, people with disabilities and Travellers and with further Census questions promised in relation to ethnicity. The data collected on these groups is being published in a valuable manner by the Central Statistics Office which has announced a series of data reports on each of the nine grounds. The first of these – *Women and Men in Ireland, 2004* – was published in December 2004.

However, there remain significant gaps in the administrative data available across the nine grounds. In 2003 the National Statistics Board published *Developing Irish Social and Equality Statistics to Meet Policy Needs.*[41] The National Statistics Board is responsible to Government for setting priorities for the compilation and development of official statistics in Ireland. The publication was prepared by a steering group which was established to undertake a scoping study of what needs to be done for social and equality statistics to meet current and impending policy needs. This report is a key initiative in supporting the development of a response to the data deficits that limit current approaches to equality mainstreaming.

The report highlights the demands for social and equality

data that flow from 'increased pressure for accountability and measurement of the success of national programmes' due to the social partnership model within policy making, from legislative and policy developments that 'create pressure for greater accountability and a need to benchmark and measure developments', from 'moves towards evidence based policy making' and from EU demands on 'domestic policy in terms of measuring progress and of meeting new targets and obligations in the social and equality spheres'. The report suggests that 'the challenge is not only a question of resources, although this is of course a major issue but is also one of finding methodologically sound and innovative means of producing relevant and accurate information'.[42]

The report emphasises the need for the further development and gathering of administrative data. It supports the 'general view that the "evidence-based" element of social policy making has typically been underdeveloped in the Irish system'. It sets out a strategy that is currently being implemented by Government Departments. Each Government Department is to establish a statistics committee of data users and data producers to determine how data needs can be met within the Department, to establish what information is required that is not internally available, to identify data needs in respect of complex and cross cutting issues and to identify how to enhance staff skills in using data in policy evaluation and development. Each Department is to devise a statistics strategy and to include this in its Statement of Strategy and to report on it in its annual report. The report identifies that there is 'a wide ranging variety of administrative data sources than can potentially generate social and equality statistics' but points to problems that flow from 'different concepts or definitions that are often used in the various databases, such as different geographical units, age bands or definitions of social group'. It recommends 'standardisation, co-ordination and classification of data collection and maintenance, so that data banks across the public service can be interrogated using a common approach'.[43]

Institutional Infrastructure

An institutional infrastructure for equality mainstreaming in the public sector will need to be further developed. This should ensure a capacity to implement equality mainstreaming to a standard that realises practical outcomes for those groups experiencing inequality and to sustain an equality mainstreaming approach into the future. This institutional infrastructure will also need further development in the future so that integrated equality and poverty mainstreaming can be implemented.

This new institutional infrastructure will need to be made up of units within Government Departments and an independent organisation external to Government Departments. This infrastructure is needed to ensure that equality mainstreaming is integral to the policy making and programme design processes of the Department and to ensure that there is an ongoing external support and stimulus for this equality mainstreaming. Small units should be established in each Government Department to support a capacity for equality mainstreaming. These should be staffed by people with an expertise in equality issues and in equality mainstreaming. The personnel in these units should have sufficient status within the Department to intervene and effectively influence equality mainstreaming in policy making and programme design. They should have strong links to the independent organisation. This independent organisation should be an expert body like the Equality Authority. This independent organisation should set standards for equality mainstreaming and should assess outcomes from this approach. It should provide practical support in terms of resource materials to assist equality mainstreaming in Government Departments.

Policy Implementation

Policy thinking, policy making and policy implementation all form parts of a policy cycle. Policy thinking encompasses the values and analysis that shape policy making. Policy making requires policy implementation. Policy implementation in turn can inform the values and analysis that make up policy thinking. Concern has been expressed by the social partners at the manner in which this policy cycle is regularly broken at the point of policy implementation. In a National Economics and Social Forum report they highlighted that 'while recognising the significant achievement of social partnership, almost all groups expressed some frustration and disappointment with the difficulty in turning participation in social partnership into real change'.[44] The targeted initiative for Traveller accommodation described earlier highlighted the issue of failure in policy implementation.

A problem solving approach to economic and social issues has emerged at national level through the various arenas of social partnership. This is most evident in the series of national agreements negotiated between the Government and the social partners. These agreements have brought a problem-solving approach to issues in policy thinking and policy making rather than policy implementation. A similar problem-solving approach could usefully be developed in relation to issues in policy implementation. This could secure a more effective policy cycle.

A problem-solving approach to policy implementation issues should be participative. The social partners could bring their knowledge, insight and information to bear on the issues in the same manner they have done in relation to issues in policy thinking and policy making. However, the problem-solving process needs to take place at local level rather than at national level, in other words at the level where most policies get implemented. The specific barriers to policy implementation will need to be identified and addressed. The approach to this should ensure that the policy thinking that shaped policy making would also shape policy implementation. Equally. the approach should ensure that the experience of policy implementation influences new policy thinking and policy making.

NOTES

1. Financial Statement of the Minister for Finance Mr Brian Cowen TD, 1st December 2004
2. Financial Statement of the Minister for Finance Mr Brian Cowen TD, 1st December 2004
3. *Submission by the Equality Authority on the Disability Bill 2004 and Comhairle (Amendment) Bill 2004*
4. *Report of the Working Group on the Review of the Parental Leave Act 1998*, Department of Justice, Equality and Law Reform (Dublin) 2002
5. Fine-Davis, M., Fagnani, J., Giovannini, D., Hoggaard, L. and H., Kluwer, *Fathers and Mothers: Dilemmas of the Work Life Balance: A Comparative study in Four European Countries*, Academic Publishers, (Netherlands) 2004
6. *Report of the Task Force on the Travelling Community*, The Stationery Office (Dublin) 1996
7. *Report of the Task Force on the Travelling Community*, The Stationery Office (Dublin) 1996
8. *Report of the Commission on Itinerancy*, The Stationery Office (Dublin) 1963
9. *Report of the Commission on Itinerancy*, The Stationery Office (Dublin) 1963
10. *Report of the Task Force on the Travelling Community*, The Stationery Office (Dublin) 1996
11. *Report of the Travelling People Review Body*, The Stationery Office (Dublin) 1983
12. *Report of the Travelling People Review Body*, The Stationery Office (Dublin) 1983
13. *Report of the Travelling People Review Body*, The Stationery Office (Dublin) 1983
14. *Report of the Travelling People Review Body*, The Stationery Office (Dublin) 1983
15. *Report of the Task Force on the Travelling Community*, The Stationery Office (Dublin) 1996
16. *Report of the Task Force on the Travelling Community*, The Stationery Office (Dublin) 1996
17. *Report of the Task Force on the Travelling Community*, The Stationery Office (Dublin) 1996
18. *A Strategy for Equality*, Report of the Commission on the Status of People with Disabilities (Dublin) 1995
19. *A Strategy for Equality*, Report of the Commission on the Status of People with Disabilities (Dublin) 1995
20. Quin, S. and Redmond, B., 'Moving from Needs to Rights: Social Policy for People with Disability in Ireland', in *Contemporary Irish Social Policy*, University College Dublin Press, 1999
21. *National Standards for Disability Services*, Department of Health and Children and National Disability Authority, (Dublin) 2004

22. *National Standards for Disability Services*, Department of Health and Children and National Disability Authority, (Dublin) 2004

23. Cullen, Delaney, Duff, *Caring, Working and Public Policy*, Equality Authority, (Dublin) 2004

24. *Mainstreaming Equality: Model for a Statutory Duty*, Conference Report, Equality Authority, (Dublin) 2003

25. *Incorporating Equal Opportunities for Women and Men Into All Community Policies and Activities*, (COM 96/67), European Union, 1996

26. McGauran, A.M and Crowley, N., *Gender Mainstreaming in Ireland – The Past and the Future*, Institute of Public Administration, (Dublin) 2005

27. *Equality Proofing Issues*, Forum Report No. 10, National Economic and Social Forum, (Dublin) 1996

28. *Partnership 2000 for Inclusion, Employment and Competitiveness*, The Stationery Office (Dublin) December 1996

29. *Programme for Prosperity and Fairness*, The Stationery Office, (Dublin) 1999

30. *Sustaining Progress*, The Stationery Office, (Dublin) 2002

31. *Partnership 2000 – Working Group Report on Equality Proofing*, Department of Justice, Equality and Law Reform and University College Cork, (Dublin) 2000

32. *Partnership 2000 – Working Group Report on Equality Proofing*, Department of Justice, Equality and Law Reform and University College Cork, (Dublin) 2000

33. *An Equality Proofing Template for the City and County Development Boards*, Equality Authority, (Dublin) 2002

34. *Equality Impact Assessment, Initial Guidelines for the City and County Development Boards*, Equality Authority, (Dublin) 2003

35. *Integrated Policy Proofing Template*, Community Legal Resources, Equality Authority, Combat Poverty Agency, Office of Social Inclusion, Department of Justice, Equality and Law Reform, (Dublin) 2004

36. *Opinion on the Recommendations to Strengthen the Implementation of the European Employment Strategy*, Advisory Committee on Equal Opportunities for Women and Men, European Commission, (Brussels) June 2004

37. *Opinion on the Recommendations to Strengthen the Implementation of the European Employment Strategy*, Advisory Committee on Equal Opportunities for Women and Men, European Commission, (Brussels) June 2004

38. *Strengthening the Implementation of the European Employment Strategy*, Communication from the Commission, 2004

39. *Opinion on the Recommendations to Strengthen the Implementation of the European Employment Strategy*, Advisory Committee on Equal Opportunities for Women and Men, European Commission, (Brussels) June 2004

40. *Gender Matters – A Consultation Document: Towards a cross-departmental strategic framework to promote gender equality for women and men 2005–2015*, Gender Equality Unit, Office of the First Minister

and Deputy First Minister, (Belfast) 2004

41. *Developing Irish Social and Equality Statistics to meet Policy Needs,* Report of the Steering Group on Social and Equality Statistics, National Statistics Board, The Stationery Office, (Dublin) 2003

42. *Developing Irish Social and Equality Statistics to meet Policy Needs,* Report of the Steering Group on Social and Equality Statistics, National Statistics Board, The Stationery Office, (Dublin) 2003

43. *Developing Irish Social and Equality Statistics to meet Policy Needs,* Report of the Steering Group on Social and Equality Statistics, National Statistics Board, The Stationery Office, (Dublin) 2003

44. *A Framework for Partnership: Enriching Strategic Consensus through Participation,* National Economic and Social Forum, (Dublin) 1997

Chapter Five

Equality Competent Institutions

Equality competence has emerged as a key concept in the developmental work of the Equality Authority. It is a concept that focuses attention on the systems and practices of an institution and their capacity to promote equality and combat discrimination. An equality competent institution requires equality competent individuals to staff it. As such it is a concept that also focuses attention on the attitudes and behaviours of individual staff. Equality competence is a goal to be achieved by all institutions in society if an ambition for equality is to be realised.

Equality competence concerns the ability or capacity of an institution to effectively pursue equality objectives. Equality objectives, as highlighted earlier, encompass access to resources, including jobs or education, accommodation or health provision, access to decision-making, access to a valuing and an accommodation of difference and access to relationships of love, care and solidarity. Equality competent institutions form a valuable part of the strategic framework for action on equality. Equally they are shaped and supported by the other dimensions to the strategic framework, such as legislation, mainstreaming and targeting.

The equality competent institution would be an institution where:

• procedures are in place to address issues of discrimination if they arise and steps are taken to prevent discrimination happening;

- a culture and a practice that values difference and diversity is established and where adjustments are made to take account of needs specific to employees and customers from across the nine grounds;
- a proactive approach to equality is pursued and where positive action is deployed in support of full equality in practice. This involves a mix of targeted initiatives and mainstreaming approaches as explored in the previous chapter.

Equality competent institutions would be characterised by a planned and systematic approach to equality. This is an approach that involves a formal institutional commitment to equality alongside staff capacity to reflect this commitment in practice. It involves clearly stated equality objectives alongside planned activities to achieve these. Equality competent institutions would also be characterised by governance that includes an equality focus. Governance is about how decisions are made within an institution. This characteristic brings an equality focus into the heart of decision making. An equality focus within governance involves the implementation of equality impact assessments, the participation of groups experiencing inequality in decision-making and the gathering and analysis of equality related data for the institution.

Equality competence is about the institution and about the individual's workings within the institutions. Institutional policies, practices, procedures and structures would be organised to contribute to the achievement of equality objectives. Individual attitudes, behaviours, skills and actions would be geared to contribute to equality objectives. Equality competence covers all nine grounds protected under the equality legislation and all areas of activity included in the scope of this legislation. It is a competence that needs to be visible in employment, service provision, planning, policy making and programme development.

An Equal Status Review

An equal status review is one important tool in achieving equality competence for an institution because it underpins and shapes a planned and systematic approach to equality. An equal status review examines the policies, practices, procedures and perceptions within an organisation for their impact on equality in service delivery for people from across the nine grounds of gender, marital status, family status, age, disability, sexual orientation, race, religion and membership of the Traveller community. Barriers to equality in service provision are identified within an equal status review and an evidence base is developed from which to identify an equality action plan that would enhance equality in service provision. Service providers, service users, advocacy groups and organisations representing groups from within the nine grounds have an input as part of this process into the manner in which services are designed and delivered so as to enhance their impact on equality.

In 2004 the then North Western Health Board (now Health Service Executive – North Western Area) implemented the first Equal Status Review and Action Plan. This was supported by the Equality Authority and the Department of Justice, Equality and Law Reform. It was conducted by an independent consultant. The review concentrated on five specific service areas – mental health services, accident and emergency services, maternity services, community welfare services and general practice services. These service areas were chosen for the fact that they involved a client base characterised by significant levels of diversity and for involving a high level of general medical service clients.

An equal status review is limited to a focus on service provision. Equality competence involves a concern with equality in both employment and service provision. This is best served by an equality review that encompasses employment and service provision. However, it was important at this early stage in promoting the concept of equality competence to test out a methodology for conducting an equal status review. This review was breaking new ground in that such a review had not been carried out before. It was necessary to explore and build an effective approach to equal status reviews. The Equality Authority was implementing a separate scheme of employment equality reviews at the same time. In the future the equal status review and employment equality review models will need to be integrated to better support equality competent institutions.

A template was developed for the equal status review in the North Western Health Board.[1] This was organised under the headings of planning, the equality infrastructure, service provision, access to services and perceptions of services. Each service area was to be examined in relation to each of these headings.

The focus on planning involved an examination of corporate strategic development and annual service plans. In the review the consultant sought to identify how equality considerations were included, managed and named within these processes. The focus on planning also involved an examination of budget preparation and resource allocation. The consultant sought to identify how equality issues were targeted within these processes.

The equality infrastructure focus involved an examination of how the organisation was actively managing the work of promoting equality, accommodating diversity and preventing discrimination in the different service areas. This required an exploration of structures and procedures to drive forward an equality focus in the organisation. The consultant examined to what extent leadership was provided on equality issues, whether an equality officer or an equality committee were in place and what roles they played if they were, how an equality focus was included in service standards and any reporting on equality issues. She sought to identify the presence and quality of equality policies and the provision and quality of equality and diversity training for staff. Data collection and analysis on health status, health service utilisation and health service outcomes across the nine grounds was also explored. Finally the consultant examined where and to what extent people and organisations from across the nine grounds were involved in planning and in decision-making on the design and delivery of services.

The service provision focus in the review involved an examination of all policies, procedures and practices governing service provision. The consultant sought to explore the extent to which these policies, procedures and practices ensured discrimination is prevented, diversity accommodated and equality promoted in mainstream service provision. She also examined services targeted on specific groups from across the nine grounds. The level and quality of these positive action initiatives were also explored and the extent to which they were integrated with general service provision.

The focus on access to services involved an examination of the physical infrastructure in the five service areas for its accessibility. It involved an examination of information materials for their accessibility and of communication strategies for their effectiveness with groups from across the nine grounds. Customer service strategies were examined for their focus on a diversity of customers and for their capacity to achieve equality objectives.

The final focus for the review involved an examination of perceptions of the services. The consultant explored the perceptions of service providers and of service users. She sought to examine how these groups viewed equality objectives and equality issues and to what extent they perceived service provision design and delivery to be shaped by equality considerations.

An early challenge in implementing the review was to establish a credibility for the equal status review process within the organisation and to secure an ownership of the process at all levels in the organisation. The consultant built this credibility through initial interviews with managers and with key staff in the five service provision areas covered by the review.

The consultant then examined documentation prepared by the health board or at national policy level on the five service areas covered. This included written policies and procedures and documented practices within these service areas. The consultant analysed any relevant equality data gathered within these service areas. This initial research provided a body of evidence for the review in terms of establishing the current situation for groups from across the nine grounds in relation to each of the service areas and in terms of how the literature and data incorporated and dealt with issues of equality and diversity.

This evidence was then further explored by the consultant through a series of structured and semi-structured interviews with managers and service providers within the five service areas, with staff and managers with specific responsibilities for equality in service provision, with senior management personnel at health board level and with managers of services specifically targeted on groups experiencing inequality. In these interviews she sought to analyse and further develop learning and insights from the literature and data examined. She explored the equality challenges facing each of the service areas, the impact of Board-wide policies and procedures on equality in service provision, equality issues specific to the service areas and future plans to promote equality in service provision.

Focus groups rather than a questionnaire were identified by the consultant as the most effective means of including the perceptions of service providers and service users in the review process. The focus groups examined equality as an issue, explored service provision for its impact on equality and supported staff and service users to identify solutions to problems identified. This participative dimension to the equal status review provided a valuable source of new information and ideas and ensured a democratic dimension to the further evolution of equality competence for the organisation.

Finally the consultant prepared a report of the review and developed an equality action plan. The equality action plan identified equality initiatives to be implemented in the areas of planning of services, provision of services, access to services and development of equality infrastructure. An extensive process of presentation to and consultation with management in the service areas and in the wider Health Board about the equality action plan was designed by the consultant to ensure its relevance and to develop a commitment to its implementation. The equality action plan included steps to make equality a corporate and strategic objective, to mainstream a focus on equality into service planning processes, to enhance participation by and consultation with client groups from across the nine grounds, to develop methods to record equality related data from across the nine grounds, to build training and awareness raising programmes for staff and to enhance the provision of accessible information.

EQUALITY COMPETENCE – PLANNED AND SYSTEMATIC
APPROACHES TO EQUALITY

This Equal Status Review is explored in some detail given the importance of this process to equality competence in institutions. Planned and systematic approaches to equality have been identified as one key characteristic of equality competent institutions. An equal status review is important in underpinning and shaping a planned and systematic approach to equality within an institution.

The concept of 'planned and systematic' has been recognised as necessary in the promotion of equality in the amended Gender Equal Treatment Directive.[2] This Directive is limited to the gender ground and to a workplace focus. It requires that Member States 'in accordance with national law, collective agreements or practice encourage employers to promote equal treatment for men and women in the workplace in a planned and systematic way'. This provides a valuable endorsement of this approach to equality and should stimulate initiatives to support and require such an approach.

Planned and systematic approaches to equality are based on formal equality policies and plans. They do not solely depend on individual good will and commitment. They focus on achieving agreed equality objectives for employees and customers or service users rather than merely reacting to incidents of discrimination or inequality. These approaches are sustained over the long term within institutions rather than being limited to ad hoc short-term actions.

Planned and systematic approaches to equality require an equality infrastructure within an organisation. This infrastructure involves:

- equality policies;
- equality and diversity training for staff;
- an equality action plan based on an equality review;
- assigning responsibility for equality within the institution.

This equality infrastructure is based on practical and agreed equality objectives for employees and customers or service users from across the nine grounds covered by the equality legislation. These objectives should encompass a holistic approach to equality that is concerned with access to employment and career progression and to services, access to participation in decision-making, access to a status and a valuing of the diversity and difference of employees and customers or service users, and access to relationships of care and solidarity.

Equality Policies

Equality policies involve institutions in setting out their broad commitment to equality for employees and customers or service users. They establish overarching principles and broad strategies to shape and implement this commitment to equality and commit institutions to preventing discrimination, sexual harassment and harassment. They need to identify procedures by which such issues will be addressed if they arise. These policies commit institutions to promoting equality through positive action, and through making adjustments for diversity, including the reasonable accommodation of people with disabilities.

The Equality Authority, IBEC and Congress have developed guidance in relation to employment equality policies.[3] This guidance sets out a number of headings for an employment equality policy. These cover organising for equality in the workplace, recruitment and job advertising, the interview process, job orientation and induction, career promotion and progression. The guidance emphasises that 'an employment equality policy can only serve as a foundation'. Practices and procedures need to be developed to implement the policy and to realise its potential. The guidance highlights: 'The communication of an employment equality policy throughout an organisation and its customer and supplier circuits is considered a priority.' The guidance sets out the case made by the Australian Human Rights and Equal Opportunity Commission for an effective anti-discrimination policy as being that it:

- reduces the likelihood of misunderstanding and confusion about the organisations' policy and procedures;
- reduces the likelihood of employer liability;
- provides a more harmonious work environment; and greater productivity.

The Equality Authority has provided guidance in relation to dealing with issues of sexual harassment and harassment in the equality policy of an organisation. The Equality Authority's Code of Practice on Sexual Harassment and Harassment at work highlights that 'prevention is the best way to minimise sexual harassment and harassment in the workplace. An effective policy and a strong commitment to implementing it is required. The purpose of an effective policy is not simply to prevent unlawful behaviour but to encourage best practice and a safe and harmonious workplace where such behaviour is unlikely to occur. This policy is likely to be more effective when it is linked to a broader policy of promoting equality of opportunity.'[4] This code of practice identifies that the policy should set out the commitment to ensuring the workplace is free from sexual harassment and harassment, should define sexual harassment and harassment and identify responsibilities to ensure that it does not occur and that complaints are addressed speedily and should set out a complaints procedure and commit to staff training on issues of sexual harassment and harassment.

Finally, in relation to equality policies, the Equality Authority's Equal Status Policy provides one model for a customer or service user focus within equality policies. This policy sets out the Equality Authority's 'commitment to meet our obligations under the Equal Status Act 2000, to proactively promote equality and to work to prevent discrimination'.[5] The policy makes commitments in relation to materials produced by the Equality Authority, reasonable accommodation of people with disabilities, reasonable accommodation of diversity across all grounds covered by the equality legislation, customer relations, customer feedback, communications strategy, organisation of events, outcomes that achieve benefits for all groups covered by the legislation, official languages equality and advertising. The policy identifies steps to communicate the policy, to train staff on the issues covered by the policy, to collect and track customer data from across the nine grounds, to deal with complaints and to keep the policy under review.

Equality and Diversity Training

Equality and diversity training is necessary to ensure the capacity of staff to implement equality policies. The Equality Authority, Congress and IBEC have developed guidance on equality and diversity training. This guidance primarily applies to employment and the workplace. It identifies that 'equality training in the workplace is usually undertaken in an attempt to develop knowledge, skills, behaviours or attitudes through learning experiences, which are carried out in a planned and systematic way in order to achieve effective performance in an activity or range of activities or to change a behaviour or a range of behaviours and thus to change or reinforce the culture of an organisation'.[6] The guidance also has a relevance to equality and diversity training that supports equality for customers or service users.

This guidance identifies that the 'training should be designed to address practical change to achieve specific goals'. These goals would relate to commitments made in the equality policy of the organisation and the equality objectives established in the equality action plan of the organisation. The guidance outlines a strategic approach to planning and implementing equality and diversity training and identifies a broad range of priority themes for the content of the training. These seek to address deficits in knowledge, awareness and skills and include:

- recruitment and selection training;
- bullying, harassment and sexual harassment training;
- training on equality legislation;
- work/life balance training;
- employment equality training for senior management and human resource personnel;
- positive action training;
- training on developing/operating equality policies and procedures;
- managing diversity skills training;
- training on serving a diverse customer base;
- equality and diversity sensitivity training in relation to each of the nine grounds.

Equality and diversity training develops new knowledge, skills and attitudes among staff. It supports an equality competence for individual staff members. Cultural change within institutions is also stimulated by such training in that it supports a culture that welcomes and values diversity and in that it supports the need for action to promote equality.

Equality Action Plan

An equality action plan provides the necessary context within which new knowledge, awareness and skills can be applied by staff within the equality competent institutions. Equality action plans set out equality objectives in relation to employment and service provision and the steps that will be taken to achieve them. Such plans need to be evidence based and are developed on foot of an equality review. The experience of the North Western Health Board in carrying out an equal status review in relation to service provision is described earlier and demonstrates an approach to be followed in this regard.

Allocation of Responsibility

A final element in this equality infrastructure is the allocation of responsibility for equality issues within the institution. This can be achieved by a senior member of staff taking on additional responsibilities in relation to equality or, in larger organisations, by the appointment of an equality officer and/or the creation of an equality committee. Equality must be the responsibility of everyone within the institution if it is to be effectively pursued. However, the effective promotion of equality also needs people with a specific expertise in relation to equality issues and with the time and resources to stimulate, support and monitor activities to promote equality.

An equality officer is an important resource within an equality competent institution. The equality infrastructure necessary for a planned and systematic approach to equality can be developed by an equality officer who also supports implementation of the activities set out in an equality action plan. The Equality Officer can respond to equality issues as they arise, can build a knowledge base for the institution on equality issues and can liaise with organisations representing groups experiencing inequality across the nine grounds. An equality committee can also be convened by the equality officer.

An equality committee brings together employer, trade union and employee, and customer representatives to support planned and systematic approaches to equality within the organisation. The membership of such an equality committee can contribute a diversity of perspectives to the development and implementation of this planned and systematic approach to equality and can thus ensure it is relevant to all staff and customers and sectors within the institution. The membership can also contribute to a consensus behind the equality objectives of the institutions and to a broad commitment to their implementation.

MEASURING PROGRESS

'Towards a Workplace Equality Infrastructure' is a survey of the extent to which an equality infrastructure is in place within institutions to support planned and systematic approaches to equality. It was carried out by Millward Brown IMS Limited and was based on a sample of 300 private sector and 100 public sector (excluding government departments) institutions.[7] It was published by the Equality Authority in partnership with IBEC, Congress, the Construction Industry Federation and 'Know Racism' (the National Anti-Racism Awareness Programme) as part of Anti-Racist Workplace Week 2002.

It found that 'less than half of all organisations have a formal written policy to deal with equality issues. In the private sector specifically, only 40% of organisations claim to have such a policy. The record is better in the public sector with 63% claiming to have a formal written policy.' This finding is a cause for concern. Employers and service providers should take reasonable steps to prevent discrimination including harassment and sexual harassment or they could be held liable in cases under the equality legislation. Such steps would include having policies and procedures in place to prevent or address such discrimination. The survey found that 'most organisations in the public (76%) and private (69%) sectors claim to have informal plans and procedures to deal with equality issues' and suggested that 'this is a limited and inadequate response'.

The survey looked beyond equality policies to the presence of other elements of an equality infrastructure within institutions. The picture that emerged was not positive. 'Only 36% of all organisations have organised awareness and training for staff while a mere 15% of all organisations have established a committee to deal with equality issues' according to the survey. It did find that '50% of all organisations have nominated a staff member to deal with equality issues'.

A fragmented approach to action taken to promote equality

and/or avoid discrimination was found within the organisations surveyed. Different sectors selected and prioritised different grounds in their promotion of equality. Public sector organisations had a particular focus on the grounds of disability, gender, race, family status and age in their activities to promote equality. In the private sector action taken related to the gender, race, age and marital status grounds. The grounds of religion, sexual orientation and Traveller community had a very limited profile in the activities of organisations in the private and public sectors. Integrated and comprehensive approaches to equality that encompass all nine grounds are not being taken up to any great extent in either the public or the private sectors.

The most developed equality infrastructure was found in public sector and large private sector organisations. The most limited development of an equality infrastructure was found in small organisations in the private sector. This identifies the need to explore the reasons for this limited development and to provide supports targeted at stimulating the development of an equality infrastructure in such organisations.

Research was carried out by the Equality Authority, IBEC and Congress within the National Framework Committee for Equal Opportunities at the Level of the Enterprise in 2003 which explored barriers to promoting equality in small and medium enterprises. This small scale research identified that equality initiatives within this sector are 'needs driven, as perceived by the employer but reactive'.[8] It identified a range of barriers within the small and medium enterprise sector to more planned and systematic approaches to equality including:

- lack of detailed knowledge of the equality legislation and fear and uncertainty in terms of what is involved and how to comply;
- perceived lack of relevance, or uncertainty of relevance, of equality policies and procedures;
- fear of what might be provoked if people are made aware of the issues;
- fear that formalizing equality plans could lead to tension, disruption and/or discontent in the workplace;
- perceived costs and lack of resources available for

development of equality infrastructure including time, expertise and finance; and related concerns regarding sustainability, particularly in small owner-managed companies.

A resistance to change was identified in this sector. Fears in relation to doing things differently to achieve equality objectives were found to be barriers to change. Access to resources and expertise would assist in dismantling these barriers. The National Framework Committee for Equal Opportunities at the Level of the Enterprise responded to these research findings by developing a grant scheme targeting small and medium sector enterprises. This provided finance for companies to buy in consultancy expertise to develop equality policies and strategies for equality and diversity training. The consultants are required to make use of the guidance developed by the committee in relation to employment equality policies and equality and diversity training. This scheme has stimulated new practice within small and medium sector enterprises that has dispelled fears and diminished resistance to change. New role models are emerging within the sector that will stimulate change beyond the small number of organisations supported by the scheme.

EQUALITY COMPETENCE – GOVERNANCE WITH AN EQUALITY FOCUS

Planned and systematic approaches to equality have been identified and described earlier as one key characteristic of equality competent institutions. A second key characteristic has been identified as a system of governance that has an equality focus. Key elements of such a system are the implementation of equality impact assessments, participative decision-making and equality data gathering and analysis. Governance is about how decisions are made within an institution. This characteristic of the equality competent institution brings an equality focus into the heart of decision-making – it holds similarities to the mainstreaming approach described in the previous chapter.

An equality impact assessment tests the capacity of a plan, budget, service or employment strategy being developed by the institution, to take account of diversity and to promote equality.

It is carried out as part of the design stage of such initiatives. The aim of the equality impact assessment is to ensure that key decisions made will contribute to equality for all groups covered by the equality legislation. An equality impact assessment is therefore key to governance that has an equality focus.

Decision making that is participative is another element of such governance systems with a focus on equality. Participative decision making involves an engagement with customers and employees from groups experiencing inequality across the nine grounds. The institution engages with the organisations that represent and articulate the interests of these groups. This engagement can involve the inclusion of those who experience inequality and their organisations in existing consultative fora. A specific dialogue between the institution and these individuals and their organisations is also necessary to identify their particular needs and how these needs can best be met within and by the institution.

This participative decision-making contributes to a democratisation of the institution and empowers those who are often otherwise marginal to institutional decision-making. It facilitates a flow of knowledge about, information on and perspectives of groups experiencing inequality into the institution that contribute to the quality of decision-making and to the equality competence of the institution. Careful consideration is required to identify the relevant organisations to engage with and to develop systems of participation that are effective and appropriate for the groups covered by the equality legislation. Participative decision-making is also usefully supported by a training and support strategy to enable staff of the institution and members of the equality organisations to participate effectively together.

The final element of governance with an equality focus is evidence based decision-making. Equality impact assessments and participative decision-making that engages with those experiencing inequality requires a flow of equality related data if such approaches are to be effective. Currently there are significant deficits in data on the identity, experience and situations of groups experiencing inequality. Data gaps persist within institutions on employment, uptake of service provision and outcomes from service provision across the nine grounds covered by the equality legislation. These deficits and gaps need to be eliminated if an equality focus is to inform and shape the strategy and business plans, the budgets and resource allocations of institutions. They need to be eliminated for institutions to more effectively establish equality objectives and to monitor progress towards reaching these.

Supporting Equality Competence

Equality competent institutions need to be developed and sustained across all sectors. Support strategies are required to enable this development and sustenance. Such support strategies can involve putting in place a support infrastructure to stimulate and resource institutions to take steps towards being equality competent. The National Framework Committee on Work Life Balance is an example of one such support infrastructure and is described below. Equality competence can also be supported by the inclusion of an equality dimension within another process of change that is being implemented by an institution or a wider sector of institutions. One example of this is the Strategic Management Initiative within the public sector and the inclusion of an equality focus within the Quality Customer Service initiative and this is described below. Equality competence can also be supported by the legislative requirements. This is evident in the fields of education, accommodation and welfare provision where the equality focus has been incorporated in legislation governing these policy areas.

The Programme for Prosperity and Fairness national agreement (2000 to 2003) committed to the creation of a National Framework Committee for Family Friendly Policies at the Level of the Enterprise. The committee is convened by the Department of Enterprise Trade and Employment and includes the Department of Finance, the Department of Social and Family Affairs, the Department of Justice Equality and Law Reform, IBEC, Congress and the Equality Authority. The national agreement identifies that 'the purpose of this National Framework will be to identify actions to be undertaken by the social partners at national level which support the development of family-friendly policies in the workplace. The focus of this activity will be to support and guide the voluntary development and implementation of family-friendly policies at the level of the enterprise.'[9] This activity was to both enhance the opportunity to reconcile work and family life, and to contribute to the effective and efficient operation of the enterprise.

The National Framework Committee was further evolved under the Sustaining Progress national agreement (2003–2006).[10] This renamed the committee as the National Framework Committee for Work Life Balance and broadened the remit of the committee to include a wider range of needs and flexibilities. Work life balance has a relevance that goes beyond those seeking to reconcile work and family life to include those seeking to reconcile work with such as caring responsibilities, cultural imperatives, personal ambitions and development, and the need for flexibilities to accommodate people with disabilities and the aspirations of older people for phased retirement.

The National Framework Committee for Work Life Balance represents one important model of support for equality competence in institutions. It provides an infrastructure with a capacity to stimulate, promote and support one specific dimension to the equality competence of institutions.

There are six different components to the work of the committee. These are focused on the issue of work life balance. However, these different components reflect the supports needed to achieve a wider equality competence of institutions. These components are:

- providing leadership – Congress and IBEC represent the key actors at workplace level, employers and employees. Congress and IBEC are in a position to lead change at enterprise level and have sought to do this by communicating with their different constituencies about the importance and value of work life balance – for business, for employees and for greater equality;
- stimulating awareness – March 1st has been identified as the Annual Work Life Balance day. This is an important moment to raise the profile of work life balance issues at national, local and enterprise level;
- providing information – the work life balance website, publications on work life balance working arrangements,

research on work life balance and regional seminars all serve to enhance the body of knowledge on work life balance issues and the flow of information on these issues into enterprises;

- funding innovation – pilot projects are funded each year, by the committee, within different organisations to test out and implement a variety of approaches to work life balance. These benefit the organisation but also provide new learning on what is effective in achieving work life balance in different sectors and types of organisation;
- making expert support available – a panel of consultants on work life balance has been established by the committee. Grants are available to enterprise to assist in contracting a consultant from the panel to support the development of work life balance initiatives within the enterprise;
- creating a supportive external infrastructure – IBEC and Congress have been resourced by the committee to develop their capacity to support their members to engage in work life balance initiatives.

This is a model similar to that developed by the National Framework Committee for Equal Opportunities at the Level of the Enterprise. Both committees form part of the supports that are needed for equality competent institutions.

A second approach to supporting equality competence is to include an equality dimension within another process of change for a sector of institutions. The Strategic Management Initiative is a major change process within the civil and public service. In April 1997 a Quality Customer Service Initiative was launched as part of the Strategic Management Initiative. The aim of this was to ensure that all government departments and offices set standards of quality service for their external customers. A key element in the initiative was the preparation and implementation of Customer Service Action Plans by government departments and offices. These were to reflect nine principles of quality customer service. These initial principles reflected a minimal focus on equality with two limited references to people with disabilities and one limited reference to minorities. This change process was not therefore initially designed in a manner that would contribute to enhancing the equality competence of institutions within the sector. This changed in 2000. New principles for quality customer service were established that included an equality/diversity principle. This emphasised that customer service action plans should:

> Ensure the rights to equal treatment established by equality legislation and accommodate diversity, so as to contribute to equality for the groups covered by the equality legislation (under the grounds of gender, marital status, family status, sexual orientation, religious belief, age, disability, race and membership of the traveller community). Identify and work to eliminate barriers to access to services for people experiencing poverty and social exclusion, and for those facing geographic barriers to services.[11]

This equality/diversity principle reflected an important enhancement of the principles to guide quality customer service. Equality was identified as a core dimension to achieving quality in customer service. The new equality/ diversity principle enabled the committee implementing the quality customer service initiative to stimulate, support and secure growth in equality competence within the service provision of government departments and offices.

A working group was established under the auspices of the committee for the Quality Customer Service Initiative to support the implementation of this equality/ diversity principle. This working group was convened by the Equality Authority and included customer service officers from a number of government departments. A support pack to assist government departments to include a focus on the equality/diversity principle in their customer service action plans was developed.[12] This support pack provided material on defining equality and diversity, on approaches to accommodating diversity, on the Equal Status Act, on preparing equal status policies, on achieving accessibility and on equality and diversity training. The working group briefed the network of Quality Customer Service Officers from a broad range of government departments and offices on how to include an equality and diversity focus in customer service action plans. It reviewed the customer service action plans for equality/ diversity commitments and supported

individual government departments and offices in the
implementation of commitments they had made under the
equality/diversity principle.

The business case for equality competent institutions has
recently been established in research in an Irish context for the
first time. *Equality at Work? – Workplace Equality Policies,
Flexible Working Arrangements and Quality of Work*[13] was
published by the Equality Authority in 2005. It was prepared by
Philip O'Connell and Helen Russell of the Economic and Social
Research Institute and was based on a survey of over five
thousand employees in Irish workplaces carried out at the end
of 2003 by the Economic and Social Research Institute for the
National Centre for Partnership and Performance. The Equality
Authority commissioned the Economic and Social Research
Institute to investigate the data from this survey from a specific
equality perspective.

The research explored the impact of formal policies on
equality and of flexible working arrangements on employee
perceptions. The presence of a formal policy on equality in the
workplace was found to be associated with lower levels of work
stress, higher levels of job satisfaction and organisational
commitment and with employees' positive perceptions of
fairness and equality within their organisations. A more varied
picture emerges in relation to flexible working arrangements.
Part-time working is found to be associated with lower earnings
and lower levels of autonomy but also with reduced levels of
work stress and work pressure. Flexible hours were found to be
associated with lower levels of work pressure and greater levels
of autonomy. Home working was found to be associated with
greater levels of work pressure and stress but also with greater
levels of autonomy. Job sharing was found to be associated with
greater levels of work stress for men and a negative effect on
autonomy.

The research concluded that:

The proactive pursuit of equality in the workplace and the

implementation of flexible working arrangements are valuable in themselves in promoting equality objectives and in accommodating diversity as well as in facilitating the achievement of work life balance. This study shows that not only do equality policies entail benefits for employees such as reduced work-related stress; they can also lead to increased job satisfaction and greater organisational commitment. To the extent that they do have these effects then equality policies may also have a positive impact on organisational performance and hence be of benefit to employers.[14]

This is an important statement of the value of equality competence in and of itself – for people and for the type of society we seek to build. It is equally an important statement of the business case for equality competence. Equality policies are a key element in planned and systematic approaches to equality. Planned and systemic approaches to equality are one core characteristic of equality competent institutions. This research clearly links equality policies positively with organisational performance. This should stimulate and drive a new focus on creating equality competent institutions across the public and private sectors.

NOTES

1. Pillinger, J., E*qual Status Review in the North Western Health Board. Review of Process and Learning*, Equality Authority. Unpublished.
2. *Parliament and Council Directive 2002/73/EC* of 23rd September 2002 Amending Council Directive 76/207/EC on the Implementation of the Principle of Equal Treatment for Men and Women as Regards Access to Employment, Vocational Training and Promotion and Working Conditions (2002) OJ L269/15
3. *Guidelines for Employment Equality Policies in Enterprises*, Equality Authority, IBEC, Congress (Dublin) 2001
4. *Code of Practice on Sexual Harassment and Harassment at Work*, Equality Authority (Dublin) 2002
5. *Equal Status Policy*, Equality Authority (Dublin). 2003
6. *Guidelines on Equality and Diversity Training in Enterprises*, Equality Authority, IBEC, Congress (Dublin) 2002
7. Millward Brown IMS Ltd, *Towards a Workplace Equality Infrastructure*, Equality Authority, Know Racism, IBEC, Congress, CIF (Dublin) 2002.
8. McNally, B. and Hegarty, M., *Promoting Equality of Opportunity in Small and Medium Sized Enterprises*, Equality Authority, IBEC and Congress (Dublin) 2003
9. *Programme for Prosperity and Fairness*, The Stationery Office (Dublin) 1999
10. *Sustaining Progress*, The Stationery Office (Dublin) 2002
11. *Support Pack on the Equality/Diversity Aspects of Quality Customer Service for Civil and Public Service*, Strategic Management Initiative Quality Customer Service and the Equality Authority (Dublin) 2001
12. *Support Pack on the Equality/Diversity Aspects of Quality Customer Service for Civil and Public Service*, Strategic Management Initiative Quality Customer Service and the Equality Authority (Dublin) 2001
13. O'Connell, P. and Russell, H. (ESRI), *Workplace Equality Policies, Flexible Working Arrangements and Quality of Work*, Equality Authority (Dublin) 2005
14. O'Connell, P. and Russell, H. (ESRI), *Workplace Equality Policies, Flexible Working Arrangements and Quality of Work*, Equality Authority (Dublin) 2005

Chapter Six

Backlash and a Faltering Ambition

'The problem seems to be one of defining the Authority's role. In the transfer of power, the Equality Authority was, by its own account, given a "greatly expanded role and functions". And that was not all that greatly expanded. The Authority has three times more staff and four times more budget to spend than its predecessor. And the doors have probably been expanded to allow their heads to get through as well. It stands to reason that something must be found for all these jobsworths and pen-pushers to do all day... But if the Equality Authority now sees its role as a broader one of "promoting equality" in whatever way it happens to see fit, then it needs to be stressed that this was not part of its function when it was established' was the marker put down as early as February 2001 by Eilis O'Hanlon in the *Sunday Independent*.[1]

Coming from the same stable, the *Evening Herald* of March 2002 called: 'Protect us from the tyranny of small minds. The Equality Authority struck another blow for the forces of interfering stupidity this week when they awarded a 72-year-old-man €1,000 after he was refused entrance to the Q Bar because of his age.'[2] It went on to state: 'What makes the Equality Authority so irritating is the way they portray themselves as sole defenders of the weak and anyone who disagrees with them as bigoted, cruel cads. We're becoming a nation of whiny, quick-to-take-offence, humourless weaklings. And a lot of that is down to the Equality Authority.'

'God be with the days when people made jokes about needing to be one legged lesbians in order to get jobs. The way it's going they'll additionally have to be obese, Asian cross dressers with a prison record who are militant trade unionists and espouse revolutionary communism,'[3] commented Ruth Dudley Edwards in the *Sunday Independent* of June 2002. This referred to recommendations by the Equality Authority to expand the grounds covered by the Employment Equality Act. Her advice was: 'In any case his plans are crazy. The new Minister for Justice should clip his wings.' Kevin Myers of the *Irish Times*, writing in June 2003 on the issue of racism, wrote: 'Media comment on this issue and allied issues of "equality" has been dominated by the priggish left, aided by the imams of the Equality Authority, who by an extraordinary dereliction of duty were allowed by the Government of the day to appoint their own inspectorate, their own prosecution service, and run their own courts. For a decade or so the equality industry enforced the rule of the politically correct through their own religious courts, in which the judges were all non lawyers and believers.'[4] Referring to the change of jurisdiction from the Equality Tribunal to the District Courts in cases of discrimination involving licensed premises, he continued: 'at least Michael McDowell has ended the absurd monopoly of power enjoyed by the Equality Agency and its self-appointed fingernail-inspectors and kneecappers.'

'But nonetheless, the so-called equality agenda trundles on, an ideology that nobody asked for, a State-sponsored behemoth that sucks in everything around it; equality to the detriment of any other conflicting ideology: sometimes equality to the detriment of basic common sense,' wrote Brendan O'Connor in the *Sunday Independent* of October 2004. (5) He concluded, 'So leave us alone. You've got your Equality Authority haven't you? Play around with that and leave the rest of us get on with the business of real life', having suggested that 'if we have to start thinking about everyone's right to equality as well, we might as well give up.'

BACKLASH

These different quotes mark out one persistent trend in media comment on equality and on the developing strategic framework for action on equality. This, of course, must not be overstated. The media have played an important role in exposing inequalities, providing informed opinion and debate on inequality and equality, and in highlighting and analysing the development of a response to these issues through the various elements to this strategic framework for action on equality. The media have afforded space to other voices that have challenged these commentators. However, any media review will identify a strand of coverage on equality issues characterised by invective, trivialisation, hyperbole and/or inaccuracy even within mainstream media. There is evidence in this of a significant and sustained backlash to the current ambition for equality.

This backlash is about people seeking to block progress on equality and therefore to maintain the status quo. The progress they seek to block is equality legislation that merely seeks to prohibit less favourable treatment of people that are members of the nine grounds. The status quo they seek to maintain is characterised by significant inequalities as outlined in Chapter One. These include unequal pay for women, high levels of unemployment for people with disabilities, inadequate accommodation for Travellers, no partnership rights for gay and lesbian couples and physical and verbal abuse of Black and minority ethnic people. It is difficult to understand this backlash when it is posed in these stark terms.

Backlash has been analysed in some depth in relation to the pursuit of equality for women. American author Susan Faludi has documented the phenomenon of backlash over the 1980s – the 'backlash decade'.[6] She highlights the range of mechanisms deployed in this backlash – 'the blistering denunciations from the "radical" right, the legal setbacks, the powerful resistance of big business, the self perpetuating myth machines of the media and Hollywood, the "neotraditional" marketing drive of the glossy magazines'. She usefully points out that it is not a once off phenomenon. It is something that has an ongoing presence but can achieve an 'acute stage' at different moments in time such that she writes of 'episodes of resurgence' in relation to backlash.

Backlash is triggered by the fear of change. It is set off 'not by women's achievement of full equality but by the increased possibility that they might win it. It is a pre-emptive strike that stops women long before they reach the finishing line'.[7] Equality strategies that have begun to benefit the few meet the barrier of backlash before their benefits can become more universal. Inequalities persist but the myth that equality has just gone too far is propagated and begins to take hold.

The backlash blames equality strategies themselves for being the source of dissatisfaction and even disadvantage. The back-lash equates talk of equality and equality initiatives with the achievement of equality. 'Beyond this celebration of women's victory, behind the news, cheerfully and endlessly repeated, that the struggle for women's rights is won, another message flashes. You may be free and equal now, it says to women, but you have never been more miserable.'[8] This contradiction is resolved by a 'prevailing wisdom' that 'it must be all that equality that's causing all that pain'.[9] In this situation a myth that equality is a completed task is perpetuated. It is in fact the current inequalities that persist that continue to generate dissatisfaction, stress and disadvantage. But the myth expands to suggest that it is 'all that equality' that is the source of dissatisfaction, stress and disadvantage. This demobilises any force for change with the insistence that the goal of equality is supposedly achieved. It goes on to demonise any such force for change as the source of the ongoing absence of well being.

Clearly backlash is a complex and problematic phenomenon. It emerges with some force at a time of potential for progress on equality objectives. It is significant in the current Irish context and must be taken into account in the design, implementation and further development of the strategic framework for action on equality.

Progress Made

Previous chapters demonstrate that progress has been made. A complex and developed strategic framework for action on equality has been put in place. This includes:

- institutions, with the establishment of the Equality Authority and of the Office of the Director of Equality Investigations –

the Equality Tribunal, and the continuing operation of the Labour Court. Initiatives in this regard also include the presence and practice of equality competent institutions in a range of different sectors;

- legislation, with the enactment of the Employment Equality Act 1998, the Equal Status Act 2000 and the Equality Act 2004 and the significant body of casework that has been developed under this legislation;
- mainstreaming, with the development of gender mainstreaming within the National Development Plan and the implementation of equality proofing initiatives under the auspices of the Sustaining Progress national agreement;
- targeting, with resources targeted on groups experiencing inequality through initiatives such as the equality for women measure of the National Development Plan, the National Disability Strategy, the Community Development Programme and the Traveller accommodation programme;
- participation, with organisations articulating the interests of those experiencing inequality participating in the national arenas for social partnership and in the new structures developed as part of the reform of local government such as Strategic Policy Committees and City and County Development Boards;
- equality agendas, with the work being done by the Department of Justice, Equality and Law Reform on a National Women's Strategy and by the Equality Authority on a report entitled *Implementing Equality for Carers*. Initiatives in this regard that are already completed include the National Action Plan Against Racism, the *Report of the Task Force on the Travelling Community*, the *Report of the Commission on the Status of People with Disabilities* and the Equality Authority reports, *Implementing Equality for Lesbians, Gays and Bisexuals* and *Implementing Equality for Older People*;
- monitoring, with the publication and ongoing implementation of the report of the National Statistics Board on 'Developing Irish Social and Equality Statistics to Meet Policy Needs'.

Despite this progress significant inequalities persist and have been documented in this and previous chapters. These inequalities are evident across the economic, political, cultural and affective domains. By way of illustration, in the economic domain a gender pay gap of 17.5% continues to disadvantage women. In 2000, 63% of older people in Ireland (in this case defined as 55 to 64 years) held less than upper second level qualifications, compared to 45% among 15- to 64-year-olds. The 2002 Quarterly National Household Survey found that, compared to a national employment rate of 70%, only about 40% of those reporting a longstanding/chronic illness or disability were in employment.

In the political domain Ireland was found in 2004 to have the eighth lowest proportion of women in the Dáil of the twenty five EU Member States at 13.3%. There is a virtual absence of people with disabilities and minority ethnic people at all levels of political representation. In the cultural domain legal recognition of same sex relationships continues to be denied to gay and lesbian couples. Negative stereotyping of young people is widely evident in public discourse. The first report of the Irish Government under the UN Convention on the Elimination of all forms of Racial Discrimination failed to affirm the ethnic identity of the Traveller community. In the caring domain the Central Statistics Office reports that in 2004 less than 1% of those describing themselves as 'Looking after home/family' were men. The work of the Equality Authority on implementing equality for carers highlights the residual role played by the State in caring situations with service provision limited to where family care breaks down or to where no family carer is available.

FURTHER EVOLUTION REQUIRED

The previous chapters have highlighted the need for a further evolution of the strategic framework for action on equality. This further evolution needs to have a particular focus on institutions to promote equality, equality legislation, equality mainstreaming and the targeting of resources on those who experience inequality.

Institutions

The functions and powers of the Equality Authority are set out in Chapter Two and the argument is made that these need to be further evolved. This evolution should include the further development of enforcement powers. Explicit powers should be accorded to the Equality Authority to seek interlocutory relief from the High Court or Circuit Court in urgent cases. In relation to functions it would be important to provide for an Equality Authority function to keep legislative and policy proposals under review in order to identify their implications for the promotion of equality and the elimination of discrimination.

Institutional development to support the promotion of equality is also necessary within Government Departments and State agencies. This should involve the creation of equality units within Government Departments and key State agencies. Such units should employ staff with an equality expertise and should support an equality dimension within policies and programmes. They should liaise with the Equality Authority in developing their work.

An institutional infrastructure to promote equality is needed at local level to mirror that at national level. A local presence for the Equality Authority is required. A local advocacy for the effective implementation of equality legislation needs to be resourced and developed. A local presence could be achieved through a partnership between the Equality Authority and Citizens Information Centres and through enhancing the resources available and roles accorded to these centres. Local advocacy could be provided through local community organisations so that all who seek redress under the legislation have access to necessary information, advice and support.

Legislation

A new generation of equality legislation is proposed in Chapter Three. This should involve an enhanced mix of an individual enforcement model and statutory duties to be proactive in pursuit of equality objectives. New statutory duties would require the public sector to have due regard to equality in carrying out its functions. They would require the private sector to be planned and systematic in its approach to equality. This would ensure the legislation could more effectively address both the experience of discrimination by the individual and the institutional patterns and systems that create and perpetuate inequalities for different groups in society.

Current provision under equality legislation needs to be evolved. The legislation is ambitious in seeking to be comprehensive in covering nine different grounds. Experience to date already points to the need to expand these grounds to include socio-economic status, criminal conviction, trade union membership and political opinion. The draft EU Constitution with its incorporation of the Charter of Fundamental Rights points to an even broader range of grounds to be covered if the ambition to be comprehensive is to be realised.

Sanctions are a key dimension to current equality legislation and to any new generation of equality legislation. New provisions are required to ensure sanctions are dissuasive, proportionate and effective. This would facilitate equality legislation to make a real impact on the persistence of discrimination and would ensure that positive outcomes for individual complainants have a ripple effect on the wider community and across the public and private sectors. Effective sanctions would also ensure that new statutory duties provided for in the new generation of equality legislation were effectively implemented into the long term by the institutions and organisations they cover.

Current legislative provision should be enhanced by extending provisions requiring a reasonable accommodation of employees and customers with disabilities across all nine grounds so that the practical implications of the diversity of each ground is taken into account in employment and in the provision of goods and services. Positive action should be required by the legislation where significant imbalances are evident for particular groups. The scope of the Equal Status Acts should also be expanded to cover not only service provision by the public sector but also the functions, other than service provision, and powers of Government Departments and statutory agencies so that the legislation better reflects the provisions of the EU 'Race' Directive.

Mainstreaming and Targeting

Mainstreaming will be significantly enhanced by the inclusion of statutory duties on the public and private sectors in equality legislation. A statutory duty could in effect be a duty to implement an equality mainstreaming approach in key decision-making processes. A statutory duty will thus ensure a standard for mainstreaming – established by an independent Equality Authority – alongside a sustainability into the long term for this approach to policy making and programme design. Mainstreaming and targeting are explored in Chapter Four.

New investment is required for the further development of mainstreaming an equality focus into decision-making in the public sector and in the private sector. An institutional infrastructure adequate to stimulate and support equality mainstreaming needs to be developed. The capacity of policy makers, programme designers and decision makers to take account of the impact of their decisions on equality objectives and on groups that experience inequality needs to be supported. Support materials to facilitate simple and effective models of equality mainstreaming need to be prepared and disseminated.

Mainstreaming needs to be accompanied by targeting within a dual strategy to promote equality. Mainstreaming without targeting fails to address legacies of discrimination and can maintain current inequalities. Targeting without mainstreaming can lead to segregation and low standards. Targeting, as with mainstreaming, should be underpinned by legislation. Legislation will ringfence resources for targeted provision to address current inequalities or to meet needs specific to a group. It will ensure that eligibility for particular services and resources is accompanied by an entitlement to these resources and services.

This targeting requires the establishment of agreed and enforceable standards for targeted initiatives. Targeting should be based on an adequate needs assessment and should be accompanied by adequate and independent advocacy services. Standards, needs assessment and advocacy are key ingredients for an effective and efficient targeting of resources on those who experience inequality.

Resources need to be targeted to support the operation of

independent organisations articulating the voice of those groups experiencing inequality. These non-governmental organisations should be provided with core funding adequate to support their participation in decision-making and their advocacy for greater equality. This funding should also allow for capacity building within communities experiencing inequality to develop the knowledge and skills people need to effectively participate in decision-making that affects them.

FALTERING AMBITION

There is a need to mobilise the different societal drivers for equality that put this strategic framework for action on equality in place. This mobilisation is necessary if the various dimensions to the strategic framework are to be strengthened and further developed. This mobilisation is required in a context of significant backlash. It is also required at a time when the ambition for equality would appear to be faltering.

Evidence of such faltering ambition for equality emerges when the various societal drivers for equality are examined. These drivers are present at national, island of Ireland and EU levels. At national level there is the political process, the social partnership process and the non-governmental organisations. At island of Ireland level there is the British Irish Agreement which forms part of the Multi-Party Agreement which was negotiated to bring about a peaceful resolution to the conflict in Northern Ireland. At EU level there is the work developed by the European Commission on foot of equality commitments in the various EU Treaties.

National Level – Political Process

The Minister for Justice, Equality and Law Reform stated in 2004: 'A dynamic liberal economy like ours demands flexibility and inequality in some respects to function. It is this inequality which provides incentives.'[10] This is an indicator of a faltering ambition for equality within the political process. This indicator is further reinforced by an examination of legislative developments in relation to the equality legislation since its enactment.

The Intoxicating Liquor Act 2003 transferred jurisdiction for cases of discrimination involving licensed premises from the Equality Tribunal to the District Court. This was the culmination of a long campaign for change in the Equal Status Act by the various vintners' organisations. The change, while not increasing the compensation available, did include some improvements on the remedies available where discrimination is found to have occurred. However, the accessibility afforded by the Equality Tribunal, including its investigative role and mediation service, has been lost to cases in this area. This has resulted in a significant drop in the number of cases being taken in relation to discrimination by licensed premises.

In March 2004 the Department of Social and Family Affairs introduced an amendment under the Social Welfare (Miscellaneous) Provisions Act 2004 to limit the definition of spouse and couple to married couple and to a cohabiting couple of the opposite sex. This amendment overturned a settlement agreed in a case supported by the Equality Authority. It allowed the Department to discriminate against same sex couples in relation to a range of non-statutory administrative schemes such as the free travel scheme.

In July 2004 the Equality Act 2004 was enacted. This sought to transpose the amended Gender Equal Treatment Directive, the 'Race' Directive and the Framework Employment Directive of the EU into Irish equality legislation. This Act did enhance the equality legislation, in particular with new definitions of indirect discrimination, harassment and sexual harassment, and positive action. Improvements were made in some of the new provisions in the Employment Equality Act. However, the Equality Act did not include any new positive duties on the public or private sectors to promote equality. It introduced new exemptions in relation to non-nationals. In some areas it appears to fall short of the minimum standards set by the EU Directives, for example in relation to ensuring that all remedies available under equality legislation were dissuasive, proportionate and effective.

In December 2004 the Disability Bill 2004 was introduced into the Dáil. There are significant limitations to this legislation including its narrow definition of disability and its failure to sufficiently ringfence resources to secure entitlements to service provision for people with disabilities.

National Level – Social Partnership Process

The social partnership process has been a valuable stimulus for the development and further evolution of the strategic framework for action on equality. The Sustaining Progress national agreement contained commitments to equality proofing, to complete the review of discriminatory grounds under equality legislation, to develop a five year National Women's Strategy and to develop a framework for social and equality statistics. The agreement committed to the 'maintenance of a strong infrastructural framework to underpin the drive to eliminate discrimination, foster equal opportunity and support mainstreaming'.[11] It has a particular focus on ten special initiatives to be undertaken during the period of the agreement. Three of these had a direct relevance to grounds covered by the equality legislation – 'Migration and Interculturalism', 'Care – Children, People with Disabilities and Older People' and 'Housing and Accommodation' which makes particular reference to special housing needs, such as for older people, people with disabilities, homeless people and Travellers.

However, there is evidence of faltering ambition within the social partnership process. New priorities are taking up attention and boundaries are emerging to the consensus on workplace equality. These boundaries are evident in the Report of the Working Group on the Review of the Parental Leave Act 1998.[12] This report identified a limited consensus on improving this legislation. It identified the areas of divergence between the social partners – and indeed between Government Departments:

- in relation to paid parental leave, the Irish Congress of Trade Unions, the National Women's Council of Ireland, the Equality Authority, the Department of Justice, Equality and Law Reform, the Department of Enterprise, Trade and Employment and the Department of Social, Community and Family Affairs recommended that parental leave should attract payment. IBEC, the Irish Cooperative Organisation

Society and the Department of Finance could not support the payment of parental leave.

- in relation to paternity leave, the Irish Congress of Trade Unions, the National Women's Council of Ireland, the Equality Authority, the Department of Justice, Equality and Law Reform, the Department of Finance, the Department of Enterprise, Trade and Employment and the Department of Social, Community and Family Affairs supported a recommendation to introduce a statutory entitlement to three days paid parental leave per child payable by employers. IBEC and the Irish Cooperative Organisation could not support the introduction of such a leave arrangement.
- in relation to duration of parental leave, the majority of the review group recommended that the duration of parental leave should be increased by four weeks. The Department of Finance and IBEC did not support this recommendation.

As a result of this review new parental leave legislation was introduced into the Dáil in December 2004 that reflected a lowest common denominator of consensus. Faltering ambition in this process of social partnership meant that the legislation did not address the need for payment during parental leave, for the introduction of paternity leave nor for the extension of duration of parental leave.

National Level – Community Sector

The decision by a wide range of groups within the community and voluntary pillar not to sign up to the Sustaining Progress national agreement had the effect of removing a number of voices articulating equality interests from the arenas of social partnership. In particular the voices specifically articulating the interests of women, people with disabilities, Travellers and other minority ethnic groups and gay and lesbian people were diminished within the social partnership arrangements on foot of this decision. These groups decided against signing up to the Sustaining Progress agreement because, in their analysis, the commitments made were inadequate to enhancing the experience and situation of the communities they represented. Further groups were added to the social partnership arrangements to fill the gap in the community and voluntary pillar left by these organisations that did not sign up to the agreement. These did include organisations of older people and of carers.

On a more positive note, there was an important response by non-governmental organisations to the faltering ambition for equality identified in the political process. An Equality Coalition has begun to form which has involved the endorsement of over forty organisations.[13] The new coalition was formed in response to the proposals for change in the Equal Status Act that were brought forward during 2003 in the Intoxicating Liquor Bill. It is convened by the Irish Council on Civil Liberties. The coalition has lobbied in relation to legislation and policy on equality issues. It has responded to the Equality Bill 2004, the Social Welfare (Miscellaneous Provision) Bill 2004, the Disability Bill 2004 and the European Commission's Green Paper on 'Equality and Non Discrimination in an enlarged European Union'. This new development could serve as a stimulus for a new ambition for equality. In this it could make a contribution similar to that of its predecessor equality coalition. This predecessor coalition involved a smaller number of groups and worked effectively in the lead up to the introduction of the current equality legislation into the Dáil during the early 1990s.

Island of Ireland Level

At an island of Ireland level the British Irish Agreement within the Multi-Party Agreement signed in Belfast in April 1998 contains an important equality commitment. The Agreement requires the Irish Government to ensure 'at least an equivalent level of protection of human rights as will pertain in Northern Ireland'.[14] The Equality Authority and the Equality Commission for Northern Ireland commissioned an expert paper from Colm O'Cinnéide, a lecturer in Law at University College London, on the implications of this requirement for the further development of equality measures for Northern Ireland and Ireland.[15] This paper highlights that 'In a number of key areas, there is a greater degree of equality protection in Northern Ireland than there is in the Republic, and where no action has been taken to ensure equivalence'. These key areas include positive duties on the public and private sector under the Northern Ireland Act and the Fair Employment and Treatment (Northern Ireland) Order 1998, partnership rights extended to transsexuals and about to be extended to gay and lesbian couples, and the scope of equality legislation which includes the ground of political opinion.

Colm O'Cinnéide concludes that 'The Agreement also imposes a binding obligation upon the Republic of Ireland to ensure that at least an equivalence of rights protection is in place south of the border as that applying in Northern Ireland. This specific obligation appears to require the strengthening and extension of some elements of anti-discrimination and human rights legislation in the Republic, as well as the introduction of some form of positive public sector equality duty.'[16]

Faltering ambition is evident in relation to this requirement of equivalence. Little attention has been paid to this requirement in the implementation of the Agreement. In the Dáil debate (Report and Final Stages) on the Equality Bill in July 2004, Willie O'Dea, at the time Minister of State in the Department of Justice, Equality and Law Reform suggested that the commitment to ensure an equivalence of human rights protection as applying in Northern Ireland did not extend to ensuring an equivalence of equality provisions. This is a problematic assertion given that equality is a core human right.

European Union Level

The European Union provides another important influence on the development and evolution of a strategic framework for action on equality in Ireland. This role dates back to Irish entry into the EU and the introduction of the Anti-Discriminatory (Pay) Act 1974 and the Employment Equality Act 1977 on foot of this. This influence has continued to the present day with the three EU equality Directives which gave rise to the enactment of the Equality Act 2004.

The publication by the European Commission of a Green Paper on Equality and Non-Discrimination in an enlarged European Union in 2004 provided an important opportunity to test the level of ambition for equality being pursued by the

European Union.[17] The Green Paper is essentially a document to stimulate consultation. It sets out the contribution made to date by the European Union in combating discrimination and promoting equality. It identifies six challenges for the future. These are:

- dealing with issues linked to the enlargement of the EU;
- implementing the legal framework;
- improving data collection, monitoring and analysis;
- EU support for practical measures to tackle discrimination;
- reinforcing cooperation with stakeholders;
- integrating the principle of non-discrimination in other policy areas.

These challenges address many of the dimensions to the strategic framework for action on equality. The Equality Authority in its submission on the Green Paper stated: 'The Green Paper could usefully serve as the basis for identifying and further developing what should be an agreed framework for action necessary to achieve societies and communities characterised by non-discrimination, an accommodation of diversity and full equality in practice.'[18] The importance of developing and expanding EU level equality legislation so that a coherent, integrated and effective body of legislation covers the gender, race, disability, age, sexual orientation and religion grounds named in the EU Treaty was emphasised. The development of integrated equality mainstreaming modelled on the current approach to gender mainstreaming was recommended as was the continuation of targeted funding programmes to combat discrimination and promote equality. The importance of equality data was highlighted as was the need to include the specialised equality bodies in each Member State in a policy dialogue with the European Commission.

However, the Green Paper contained a somewhat downbeat assessment of future perspectives. In this it reflected some faltering of ambition for equality at this important EU level. It highlighted that 'enlargement will change the political and institutional context for policy making on non-discrimination and equal treatment. In the absence of an amendment to Article 13 of the EC Treaty, the adoption of Community legislation in this area continues to require unanimous agreement by Member States in the Council. This will clearly be more difficult to achieve in an EU of 25 or more Member States.'[19] It pointed out that 'much remains to be done in order to ensure the full and effective implementation and enforcement of the Racial Equality and Employment Equality Directives' and suggested that while acknowledging demands for further legislative action 'the Commission is concerned to ensure effective implementation of the current legal framework.'

In his first public address after his appointment as Commissioner for Employment, Social Affairs and Equal Opportunities, Vladimir Spidla announced a feasibility study on the extension of the current EU equality Directives and the publication by the end of 2005 of a Commission Communication on non-discrimination and equal treatment. The outcomes from these two commitments will provide the key test of the level of ambition for equality within the institutions of the European Union. This will have a key influence on any evolution of the Irish strategic framework for action on equality.

A note of concern has, however, already been sounded by David Begg, general secretary of the Irish Congress of Trade Unions, in relation to the policy direction being established by the new European Commission under the presidency of Mr José Manuel Barroso. The central development strategy for the European Union, the Lisbon Strategy, rests on three interlinked pillars each of which was to be accorded equal priority – economic, social and environmental. The objective was to make Europe the most dynamic knowledge-based economy in the world by 2010 with more and better jobs. However, progress has been slow in achieving this objective and there is evidence of shifting priorities. David Begg writing in the *Irish Times*, highlighted that 'Mr Barroso is intent on shifting policy in Europe firmly to the centre right, a long way from the Social Europe envisioned by Jacques Delors' and concluded that 'What Mr Barroso appears to be saying is "Forget social policy and the environment, focus on pro-growth, pro-business policies, cut regulation and create more jobs – but don't worry too much about the quality of those jobs"'.[20] This rebalancing of priorities in a manner that diminishes the social dimension does not bode well for the development of a strategic framework for action on equality at EU level.

In 2005 the European Union decided on new guidelines for the employment policies of the Member States.[21] These guidelines marked a new departure in the EU Employment Strategy in that they are integrated with the Broad Economic Policy Guidelines of the EU. This integration is designed to reflect an increased EU focus on jobs and growth. The new employment guidelines do state that 'Equal opportunities, combating discrimination and gender mainstreaming are essential for progress.' Targets continue for a 60% employment rate for women and 50% employment rate for older people. Eight guidelines are established. Two of these make reference to women and to gender gaps. Two guidelines refer to older people and 'low employment rates of older workers'. One guideline makes reference to 'employment for disabled people' and 'integrating migrants and minorities'. This, however, reflects a notable diminution in the focus on equality in the EU Employment Strategy. There are no guidelines dedicated to equality and non-discrimination in the labour market as had been the case prior to this within the EU Employment Strategy. The gender mainstreaming requirement, which had been an important element of the EU Employment Strategy to date, receives no more than a passing mention. The centrality accorded to equality and diversity as underpinning all the objectives of the EU Employment Strategy is no longer given any mention. The new guidelines provide significant evidence of a faltering ambition for equality at EU level.

Conclusion

Important progress has been made in constructing and applying a strategic framework for action on equality. However, discrimination demonstrates a persistence despite this progress. Inequality continues to be the experience and situation for a broad range of groups. Progress in achieving equality outcomes for these groups has been slow and limited. Yet the threat of change and further progress has stimulated significant backlash. The present context is also characterised by an ambition for equality that is clearly faltering.

There is no faltering of ambition for equality among those who experience inequality. Ambition is fuelled by anger and frustration. The voice of these groups will be the necessary foundation for the new ambition necessary to evolve the various dimensions to the strategic framework for action on equality and to enhance the impact of the strategic framework on discrimination and inequality. This voice of groups experiencing inequality needs to be supported. The key support required is finance which should be made available through state sector funding programmes. This funding also needs to be made available through independent funding sources such as trust funds or private sector funds. Resources are required to build the necessary capacity, knowledge and skills for the voice to be deployed effectively and to reflect solidarity across all groups experiencing inequality. The absence of such resources will limit and diminish the voice of groups experiencing inequality and the role that could be played by this voice in renewing and shaping an ambition for equality.

It will be important to identify and develop the spaces where progress on equality is possible. These will change over time but currently three such spaces emerge as a priority focus for action on equality. The first such space relates to the full and effective implementation of equality legislation in place. Resources need to be made available through state sector funding programmes so that those who experience inequality can make full use of the protections and rights already in place to achieve change in their experience and situation. Those who experience inequality need access to adequate information and knowledge about the equality legislation. A culture needs to be stimulated where it is deemed normal to seek to demand and exercise one's rights. Those who experience inequality need access to advocacy supports to inform, advise and resource them in seeking redress under the equality legislation.

The second such space relates to voluntary schemes of equality proofing or mainstreaming in public and private sector organisations. Equality proofing needs to be developed and resourced as a practice that is integral to policy making, programme design and the delivery of service provision. Enterprises and organisations need to be stimulated and resourced to conduct employment equality reviews and equal status reviews and to develop and implement equality action plans on foot of these. The Equality Authority has a key role to play in providing such supports and resources. However, an enhanced role for the Equality Authority in these areas will require new resources – both human resources and financial resources – being made available to the Equality Authority.

The third such space relates to institutional practice and systems. Institutions, organisations and enterprises need to be supported to be equality competent. Support is required to put in place the equality infrastructure necessary within institutions for planned and systematic approaches to equality. Governance within institutions needs to be resourced to include a focus on equality issues. The framework committees established by the social partners under the Sustaining Progress Agreement – the Framework Committee for Work Life Balance at the Level of the Enterprise and the Framework Committee for Equal Opportunities at the Level of the Enterprise – have demonstrated a valuable capacity to resource and support the development of this equality competence. It will be important that these initiatives are continued and further developed and financed into the long term beyond the current national agreement.

These are the spaces through which further progress on developing the strategic framework for action on equality can be built. Those who share an ambition for equality are present across all sectors – political, statutory, employer, trade union, trade association and community and voluntary sectors. The advocacy of these people and the solidarity they have generated within their sectors for those who experience inequality will continue to be key in providing the necessary support for this progress. Through this advocacy and solidarity they will contribute to countering the backlash and reviving faltering ambition and creating new spaces for a further evolution in the strategic framework for action on equality.

NOTES

1. O'Hanlon, Eilis, 'A New Age of Busybodies and Penpushers', *Sunday Independent*, February 18th 2001
2. *Evening Herald*, March 23rd 2002
3. Dudley Edwards, Ruth, 'The Equality Industry has Gone Mad', *Sunday Independent*, June 2nd 2002
4. Myers, Kevin, 'An Irishman's Diary', *Irish Times*, June 4th 2003
5. O'Connor, Brendan, 'Political correctness in Newspapers Equals a Load of Old Cobblers, Guv'no', *Sunday Independent*, October 17th 2004
6. Faludi, Susan, *Backlash: The Undeclared War Against Women*, Chatto and Windus, (London), 1991
7. Faludi, Susan, *Backlash: The Undeclared War Against Women*, Chatto and Windus, (London), 1991
8. Faludi, Susan, *Backlash: The Undeclared War Against Women*, Chatto and Windus, (London), 1991
9. Faludi, Susan, *Backlash: The Undeclared War Against Women*, Chatto and Windus, (London), 1991
10. In an interview with Herman Kelly, *Irish Catholic*, May, 2004
11. *Sustaining Progress: Social Partnership Agreement 2003–2005*, Stationery Office, (Dublin) 2003
12. *Report of the Working Group on the Review of the Parental Leave Act 1998*, Department of Justice, Equality and Law Reform, Stationery Office, (Dublin), 2002
13. *Towards an Equality Coalition: Proposals for Building an Equality Coalition in the Republic of Ireland*. An Equality Consultancy Brief, Irish Council for Civil Liberties, January 2005
14. Agreement Reached on the Multi-Party Negotiations, Con 3883, 1998, 37 I.L.M. 751 (1998)
15. O'Cinnéide, Colm, *The Implications of the Multi-Party Agreement for the Further Development of Equality Measures for Northern Ireland and Ireland*, Equality Authority and Equality Commission for Northern Ireland, unpublished 2005
16. O'Cinnéide, Colm, *The Implications of the Multi-Party Agreement for the Further Development of Equality Measures for Northern Ireland and Ireland*, Equality Authority and Equality Commission for Northern Ireland, unpublished 2005
17. *Equality and Non-Discrimination in an Enlarged European Union*, Green Paper, European Commission, (Brussels), 2004
18. *Building a Strategic Framework for Equality at European Union Level*, Equality Authority, (Dublin), 2004
19. *Equality and Non-Discrimination in an Enlarged European Union*, Green Paper, European Commission, (Brussels), 2004
20. Begg, David, 'Barroso Intent on Shifting EU to Right of Centre', *Irish Times*, February 7th 2005
21. *Integrated Guidelines for Growth and Jobs (2005–2008)*, Com (2005) 141 final, Brussels 2005

Index